Deceiving by Signs

Also available

Eat, Drink, and Be Merry
Stand Still and Consider
A Lamp on a Lampstand

Deceiving by Signs
A Study of Power, Signs and Lying Wonders in the Bible

By Lucas Doremus

First published 2022

Copyright © 2022 by Lucas Doremus

All rights reserved. No part of this publication may be reproduced, stored, or transmitted in any form or by any means, electronic, mechanical, photocopying, recording, scanning, or otherwise without written permission from the publisher. It is illegal to copy this book, post it to a website, or distribute it by any other means without permission.

All Scripture quotations taken from the New King James Version.

First edition

Introduction	1
Who is doing the signs?	5

SATAN

Chapter 1	11
Satan's Beginning	
Chapter 2	17
Satan's End	
Chapter 3	21
Satan in the Old Testament	
Chapter 4	25
Satan in the Gospels	
Chapter 5	33
Satan in the Church Age	
Chapter 6	37
Satan in the Eschaton	

SATAN'S POWER

Chapter 7	45
Satan's Power in the Garden	
Chapter 8	51
Satan's Power of Influence	
Chapter 9	55
Satan's Power over Job	
Chapter 10	57
Satan's Power in the Gospels	
Chapter 11	63
Satan's Power in the Church Age	
Chapter 12	69
Satan's Power in the Eschaton	

Chapter 13   73
Our Defense Against Satan's Power

DEMONS

Chapter 14   81
The Demons' Beginning
Chapter 15   83
The Demons' End
Chapter 16   85
Demons Before the Flood
Chapter 17   93
Demons in the Old Testament
Chapter 18   101
Demons in the Gospels
Chapter 19   105
Demons in the Church Age
Chapter 20   107
Demons in the Eschaton

DEMONIC POWER

Chapter 21   117
Divination, Dream Interpretation, Soothsaying, and Curses
Chapter 22   137
Magic, Sorcery, and Witchcraft
Chapter 23   151
Mediums, Spiritists, Necromancy, and Familiar Spirits
Chapter 24   155
Astrology
Chapter 25   159
Demon Possession

Chapter 26   171
Doctrine of Demons
Chapter 27   175
Judgment for Abominations in the Old Testament
Chapter 28   179
Demonic Power in the Eschaton

MODERN POWER, SIGNS, AND WONDERS

Chapter 29   187
Aliens and Extra Terrestrial Life
Chapter 30   193
Cryptozoology
Chapter 31   195
Magic in Entertainment
Chapter 32   199
Modern Rituals of Divination and Magic
Chapter 33   203
Transhumanism
Chapter 34   205
Meditations, Visions, and Remote Viewing
Chapter 35   209
Chi/Qi/Ki and Vital Energy
Chapter 36   213
Psychics
Chapter 37   215
Modern Demon Possession
Chapter 38   217
Satanic Worship
Chapter 39   219
Disease and Mental Illness
Chapter 40   221
Natural Disasters

Chapter 41 223
Sexual Desires and Sex with Demons
Chapter 42 225
Influence on Government
Chapter 43 227
Evil Places and Sites

DECEPTION OF GOD'S TRIBULATION JUDGMENTS

Chapter 44 233
Deception of the Seals
Chapter 45 237
Deception of the Trumpets
Chapter 46 241
Deception of the Bowls

Conclusion 245

To my sons, my nieces and nephews, and my friends' children,

You are growing up in a world more deceptive than the one I was raised in. May God bless you with wisdom and discernment to stand in His truth.

Introduction

Power, signs, and wonders from God are very common occurrences throughout the Bible. In fact, the Bible begins with a wonder from God: "In the beginning, God created...". Through all of creation He showed His power, and references to the Creator are found often throughout the Bible. He gave signs to His people— whether it was Noah, Abraham, Israel, the disciples, or the Church— so that they would trust in Him.

There are also other entities able to perform signs: Satan and his demons perform signs and wonders mimicking God's power. Their power is not comparable to God's, but is very effective in deceiving mankind to not trust in their Creator. Satan showed his power of deception in Genesis 3 when he deceived Adam and Eve into doing the one and only thing God told them not to do, and he will deceive mankind until he no longer can.

Satan and his demons are not mentioned very often in the Old Testament, but we know they are present and working against God's people. The New Testament mentions them more frequently as Jesus and the early Church seem to have dealt with them more directly. Satan and demons are referenced many times in the Tribulation, both through their deception and power during those seven years.

This pattern indicates a crescendo of Satan's influence until Jesus' return and then once more after the Millennium. During the Tribulation, there will be no more subtlety by Satan in his attempts to deceive the nations; it will be very direct and open for anyone to see. Yet, at the same time, his deception will be so strong that most people will not realize they are being deceived into worshiping the devil, or if they do realize they are not worshiping God, they will not change their mind because they would rather not worship the Creator (Revelation 16:11).

Revelation says of the False Prophet,

> He performs great signs, so that he even makes fire come down from heaven on the earth in the sight of men. And he deceives those who dwell on the earth by those signs which he was granted to do in the sight of the beast, telling those who dwell on the earth to make an image to the beast who was wounded by the sword and lived.
> *Revelation 13:13-14*

During the Tribulation, the False Prophet will perform signs in order to deceive the world into creating the image of the Beast and worshiping it. There will also be three unclean spirits performing signs at the time of the sixth bowl judgment to gather the Antichrist's kings for the battle of Armageddon (Revelation 16:13-16). This is the only mention in the Bible of demons directly performing signs; all other mentions of their signs are performed through humans. Why is this the only time in the Bible that demons perform signs without a human intermediary?

My guess is that God restrains evil very little if at all during the Tribulation. Jesus indicates God only restrains evil by

Introduction

shortening the Tribulation to seven years so that every human will not die "for the elect's sake" (Matthew 24:22). If there is so little restraint of evil, that means Satan and the demons' power to perform signs and wonders will be greater than ever before.

The purpose of this book is to look at the power, signs, and wonders of Satan and demons throughout the Bible and then infer what the Church may see as we grow closer to the Rapture and Tribulation. We do not want Satan to "take advantage of us; for we are not ignorant of his devices" (II Corinthians 2:11).

Studying Satan's power, signs and wonders equips us to determine the truth of supernatural signs we may encounter. If we are able to discern between signs from God and signs from Satan, we are less likely to be deceived. In fact, the first thing Jesus says about the Tribulation when asked by the disciples what will be the sign of His coming was, "Take heed that no one deceives you" (Matthew 24:4).

If we are not deceived, we are able to live a more holy life because knowing the truth makes us free (John 8:32). Not only will our life be more pleasing to God, but we can preach the Gospel to those who are deceived more effectively because we can address signs and wonders they have seen that deter them from putting their faith in Jesus. God "desires all men to be saved and to come to the knowledge of the truth" (I Timothy 2:4). Any chance to tell someone the truth about the supernatural could lead to a conversation about the Gospel. Jesus rising from the dead was a supernatural event— a sign. If you are discussing Satan's signs, there should almost always be a way to direct the conversation to the greatest sign there ever was: Christ dying on the cross for our sins and rising from the grave on the third day. And that is the only sign that must be believed to go to heaven.

Who is doing the signs?

Whenever we speak about signs, wonders, miracles, or whatever word we choose, what we mean is an occurrence in reality not fitting within God's created rules of reality. Some of the most well known examples of signs in the Bible are: bread does not multiply when you break it (Luke 9:12-17), virgins do not have babies (Luke 1:26-35), and people do not rise from the dead (Matthew 28:6). In these cases, God is the Originator of the power of the sign. We know this because all signs pointing us to glorify God must be from Him. He will not share His glory with another (Isaiah 42:8).

What we also find in the Bible are signs from a power not originating with God. These signs attempt to distract from God to bring glory to someone else, even though in the end God's judgment of those who try to take glory from Him glorifies Him (God always wins!). From where or whom does the power originate to perform these signs? Some humans claim to be the source of this power, but are they?

The Bible talks about men being able to performs signs, but in some cases it mentions they have been granted power to perform signs, such as Revelation 13:15. Who granted that power? Or did it need to be granted? In the case of the magicians of Egypt, Scripture says they were able to turn their rods into serpents "with their enchantments" (Exodus 7:11). Not every verse about men performing signs mentions the granting of power or using enchantments, but we can infer that if men or women try to perform a sign, there is something they must do to make the sign happen. They cannot simply think of the sign they want to perform and it happen. If that is so, what must they do before the sign and why does it work?

For signs from God, we know the believer must be working in accordance with God's will. Paul was able to heal the sick by God working miracles through him (Acts 19:11-12), but he also could not heal everyone since he left Trophimus sick in Miletus (II Timothy 4:20). Why couldn't Paul use the same methods to heal everyone he encountered?

Jesus said, "If you ask anything in My name, I will do it" (John 14:14) and made a similar statement in John 15:16: "Whatever you ask the Father in My name He may give you." Assuming Paul tried to heal Trophimus, surely Paul would have prayed in Jesus' name for Trophimus to be healed from his sickness. Why didn't it work?

John gives us this insight in I John 3:21-22 about receiving what we ask from God: "Beloved, if our heart does not condemn us, we have confidence toward God. And whatever we ask we receive from Him, because we keep His commandments and do those things that are pleasing in His sight." We receive what we ask for because we keep God's commandments. Keeping His commandments means we will ask for things aligning with what He wants. Even if we ask for something He does not want, we should always end our request with, "Nevertheless not My will, but Yours, be done" (Luke 22:42). In this way, we are always asking for the right thing because we are trusting God to provide for our requests.

If that is so, the power to do signs originating from God must align with His will and then He grants us the ability to perform the sign. Does it work the same way with signs not originating from the power of God? Of course, the person performing the sign doesn't have to align with God's will. But with whose will does he or she have to align? There would only be one other entity or group of entities possessing the power to grant humans the ability to perform signs and wonders: Satan and his demons.

In order to understand what Satan and demons are capable of, we must study both their character and ability throughout the Bible. Once we have a foundation for their power and motivations, we will be equipped to discern signs we see today and tomorrow. We can also share our knowledge with others to help them discern signs, always with the focus of sharing the Gospel and keeping everyone from being deceived.

SATAN

Chapter 1

Satan's Beginning

We first meet Satan in the Garden of Eden in Genesis chapter 3. "But wait," you may say, "Nowhere in the text does it say Adam and Eve were talking to Satan." That is true, but Revelation 12:7-9 talks about a great battle in which the dragon and his angels were cast out of heaven. Who is the dragon? "So the great dragon was cast out, that *serpent of old*, called the Devil and Satan, who deceives the whole world" (Revelation 12:9, emphasis added). Because the serpent in the garden is the only "serpent of old," we can identify the serpent in Genesis 3 as Satan.

But previous to Genesis 3, God called His creation "very good" in Genesis 1:31. I take this to mean there was no sin in all of creation, including the heavens and the earth. When we meet Satan in the form of a serpent, he is trying to deceive Adam and Eve into sinning against God by breaking His one and only command of what not to do: "But of the tree of the knowledge of good and evil you shall not eat, for in the day that you eat of it you shall surely die" (Genesis 2:17). What happened to Satan in between the proclamation that all of creation was very good and him trying to deceive the first humans?

Isaiah 14 and Ezekiel 28 describe what happened to Satan before Genesis 3. "But wait," you may say again, "In both passages God is addressing an earthly king." Again, that is true, but the way God is talking to and describing the entity He is addressing cannot be a human. The entity is described as an anointed and covering cherub (Ezekiel 28:14, 16). Cherubs are the creatures guarding the tree of life with a flaming sword after Adam and Even were driven out of the garden (Genesis 3:24) and the creatures on the Ark of the Covenant and in the temple in Jerusalem (Exodus 25:18, I Kings 6:23). This tells us the entity God is talking to in Ezekiel is not an earthly king.

This cherub is described as being "in Eden, the garden of God," "on the holy mountain of God," and walking "back and forth in the midst of fiery stones" (Ezekiel 28:13, 14). Later, the cherub would fall "from heaven" (Isaiah 14:12) which means he had to be in heaven at some point. This entity is said to be "the seal of perfection," have "every precious stone" as a covering, "full of wisdom," "perfect in beauty," and "perfect in your ways" (Ezekiel 28:12-15). Not only that, but this cherub was created and established by God (Ezekiel 28:14-15). This magnificent being is given the name Lucifer and Son of the Morning or literally Day Star in Isaiah 14:12.

Unfortunately, the passage does not stop at the magnificent description of this cherub God created: iniquity was found in him (Ezekiel 28:15). Lucifer said five things in his heart:

> I will ascend into heaven,
> I will exalt my throne above the stars of God;
> I will also sit on the mount of the congregation on the farthest sides of the north;
> I will ascend above the heights of the clouds,
> I will be like the Most High.
> *Isaiah 14:13-14*

Satan's Beginning

These are very different statements from Jesus' prayer in the garden of Gethsemane when He said, "Nevertheless not My will, but Yours, be done" (Luke 22:42) or when John the Baptist said, "He must increase, but I must decrease" (John 3:30). Lucifer's own heart was lifted up instead of lifting up God.

A common question asked about this event goes something like, "Why did God allow Satan to sin?" Satan and all the heavenly beings must have a free will at least similar to ours even though they are not made in the image of God as humans are (Genesis 1:26-27). God must be glorified by giving His creatures free will to choose to love Him rather than forcing His creations to love Him. Love by definition is not forced or without choice. God "first loved us" and by giving us free will, we are able to love Him back (1 John 4:19).

There isn't a direct verse saying God loves the angels but by inference He clearly does. Talking specifically about Lucifer, God loved him enough to create him with all his splendor and beauty. Lucifer was among the angels that praised Him during creation (Job 38:7). Therefore Lucifer, at one time, must have loved God back. So why did God allow him to sin? Because He loved Lucifer enough to give him free choice just like He loved Adam and Eve and gave them free will.

But why did Lucifer use his free will to sin? "Your heart was lifted up because of your beauty; you corrupted your wisdom for the sake of your splendor" (Ezekiel 28:17). How interesting that Lucifer was corrupted because of the beauty and splendor with which God created him. What a lesson to us that we must not let the gifts, talents, looks, or whatever God gives us to become something we try to exalt about ourselves instead of using those gifts to exalt the One who bestowed them on us.

But is this passage talking about Satan? At this point we are assuming it does, but the only names we have defined thus far for Satan are dragon, serpent, and devil; none of those appear in these passages. What happened to Lucifer after iniquity was found in him? He was cast "as a profane thing out of the mountain of God," destroyed "from the midst of the fiery stones," and "cast to the ground" (Ezekiel 28:16-17). All of these statements are a way of saying he fell from heaven (Isaiah 14:12). Jesus even said, "I saw Satan fall like lightning from heaven" (Luke 10:18). After all of this, what did Lucifer do?

He went and "weakened the nations" as well as defiled his sanctuaries (Isaiah 14:12, Ezekiel 28:18). Why is Lucifer doing these things? Because of the five "I will" statements that he made in his heart (Isaiah 14:13-14). In I Timothy 3:6-7, we are told an elder should not be a novice in the faith, "lest being puffed up with pride he fall into the same condemnation as the devil" and to "have a good testimony among those who are outside, lest he fall into reproach and the snare of the devil." Lucifer's pride led him to try to be like God, which means he wants to rule over all creation. Lucifer became *the* opponent of God. Therefore he is doing everything he can to rule God's creation because he believes that will bring him the most splendor and exalt his throne above God.

Now that we know Lucifer is trying to take over and rule the world as well as all creation, do we see Satan doing the same thing? In Revelation 13, we see the dragon, who we know is Satan, giving power and authority to a beast. The beast is wounded and healed, and this causes the world to marvel and follow the beast. The world in turn "worshiped the dragon who gave authority to the beast" (Revelation 13:4). Isn't this worship exactly what Lucifer wanted?

After Jesus returns in Revelation 19, an angel with a great chain

> Laid hold of the dragon, that serpent of old, who is the Devil and Satan, and bound him for a thousand years; and he cast him into the bottomless pit, and shut him up,

and set a seal on him, so that he should deceive the nations no more till the thousand years were finished.
Revelation 20:2-3

What was Satan deceiving the nations to do? Worship him (Revelation 13:4), which is exactly what Lucifer wanted (Isaiah 14:13-14). Satan and Lucifer must be the same entity because both names are used to describe a being with the goal of gaining worship from humans. There is no other indication in Scripture of another being with this goal. This means God and Lucifer are at odds with one another, both with the goal of ruling the earth and having humans worship them. Satan's method is to destroy, deceive, and weaken the nations so that they will worship him. God has a very different method.

God is not a destroyer or a deceiver, nor does He want to weaken the nations to receive worship like Lucifer does. Instead, He sent His Son to die for humans, which provided grace and mercy so that we would trust in Him. Through believing in Jesus, we give God worship. Who would you rather follow? A deceiver and destroyer or the Provider of grace and mercy? This is an easy choice for me!

But why did humans need grace and mercy? Because we sinned against God the Creator and broke His commands. When God gave Adam and Eve a command in Garden of Eden, He told them they would die if they ate from the wrong tree. If Adam and Eve never ate from the tree of the knowledge of good and evil, God would never have had a reason to execute His judgment. If they ate from the tree and God didn't have Adam and Eve die, He would have lied about them dying which would make Him a deceiver like Lucifer. Therefore, if Adam and Eve were to eat from the tree, God must execute His judgment in order for Him to be truthful.

Unfortunately, Adam and Eve did eat from the tree. But why did they do it? Where did the idea come from that it would be better to disobey God than to do what He said? That brings us all the way back to the serpent in the Garden, which we now know is Satan/Lucifer.

Adam and Eve were still perfect at the time they had this fateful conversation with Satan. The thoughts of Lucifer in Isaiah 14 must have happened before this interaction or else he would not be trying to deceive Adam and Eve into breaking God's command. If this is the case, where did sin originate?

Sin originated in the heart of Satan while he was still in Heaven. John even tells us that "He who sins is of the devil, for the devil has sinned from the beginning" (I John 3:8). It is strange to think sin originated near God's throne because we generally think of God not allowing sin in His presence. According to Job 1 and 2 as well as Zechariah 3, apparently Satan still has access to Heaven to speak with God even though he was cast out of Heaven (Ezekiel 28:16-18). Satan brought his sin with him to earth, where he began his deception of mankind.

Chapter 2

Satan's End

We will discuss the methods Satan used to deceive Adam and Eve in another chapter, but for now we know Satan was successful at influencing Adam and Eve to break God's command. Because of this God cursed Satan, telling him, "I will put enmity between you and the woman, and between your seed and her Seed; He shall bruise your head, and you shall bruise His heel" (Genesis 3:15). God revealed His plan to defeat Satan as soon as He addressed the deception Satan used with Adam and Eve.

There will be hostility between Satan and the woman, which seems to be a way to picture all mankind in contention with Satan. Then God says the same enmity will be between Satan's seed and the woman's Seed. The woman's "Seed" is a specific child from the woman, which seems incorrect because women have no seed; the seed comes from the man when a child is conceived. This is a prophecy of the virgin birth of Jesus Christ because He is the only Person to be born without seed from a man. This Seed will bruise Satan's head, which means He will defeat him. John tells us in the New Testament, "For this purpose the Son of God was manifested, that He might destroy the works of the devil" (I John 3:8).

However, Satan will also bruise the Seed's heal; that is to say the serpent will do damage to Jesus through the crucifixion and the agony preceding it. The bruising of Jesus' heal has already happened and Satan was defeated at the cross, yet Jesus has not taken His rightful place as King of the world yet. He is currently sitting down "at the right hand of God, from that time waiting till His enemies are made His footstool" (Hebrews 10:12-13).

We see this same defeat and judgment of Lucifer in Ezekiel 28: he was cut down to the ground, devoured by fire, turned to ashes, and turned into a horror (Isaiah 14:12, Ezekiel 28:18-19). If all of these things were done in the past (each judgment is in the past tense), then why do we not see Satan's defeat until after the Millennium (Revelation 20:10)? God is able to speak of "things which do not exist as though they did" (Romans 4:17). This means Satan's defeat is sure, and, according to God, it has already happened. God does not live inside time, so even though it hasn't happened in human history, it has already happened according to God. We can be thankful Satan's defeat is sure and the "God of peace will crush Satan" under our feet shortly (Romans 16:20)!

One detail in Genesis 3:15 we have not discussed is the enmity between Jesus and Satan's seed. Who is Satan's seed? Satan does not seem to have literal progeny, although this may be possible given the events of Genesis 6 which we will study in a later section. But if he doesn't have literal seed and the woman had a literal child, who is/are the seed? The best explanation I can give is Satan's seed is anyone who follows him and carries out his will, demons or humans. Jesus says of the Pharisees, "You are of your father the devil, and the desires of your father you want to do" (John 8:44). Satan did not literally provide seed for these men to be born, yet he is their spiritual father just as God is our spiritual Father when we believe in Christ. Anyone who does not believe and follows Satan instead, willingly or unwillingly because "the whole world lies under the sway of the wicked one" (I John 5:19), is hostile toward God because of their carnal mind "for it is not subject to the law of God, nor indeed can be" (Romans 8:7). In this way, there is always enmity between Satan's seed—unbelievers and demons—and Jesus.

Because of God's prophecies and declaration of judgment upon Satan, there is no salvation plan for him. Satan's decision to rebel against God cannot be revoked, for the everlasting fire has been "prepared for the devil and his angels" (Matthew 25:41).

Interestingly, we can also see from this verse that hell was created for Satan and his demons, not humans. God does not want us to go there, but be turned "from the power of Satan to God, that they may receive forgiveness of sins and an inheritance among those who are sanctified by faith" in Jesus (Acts 26:18).

Chapter 3

Satan in the Old Testament

We have seen Satan's beginning and end, but what has he been doing and what will he do in between those events? After Genesis 3, the next time Satan is mentioned chronologically in the Bible is at the beginning the book of Job. In Job chapters 1 and 2, we learn Satan has some sort of access to be able to talk with God. Satan is said to be presenting himself along with the sons of God to God (Job 1:6). We aren't told if this meeting is God calling Satan or Satan going to God of his own volition.

During the meeting, God questions Satan's actions on earth. Satan gives his report that he has been "going to and fro on the earth, and from walking back and forth on it" (Job 1:7, 2:2). God then speaks of the righteousness of Job (Job 1:8, 2:3) and Satan proceeds to argue with God about the reason for Job's righteousness (Job 1:9-11, 2:4-5). What does this indicate about what Satan is doing while he is "going to and fro?" Besides deceiving the world into worshiping him, he must be going throughout the earth finding reasons to accuse those who are righteous. But accuse them of what?

In Zechariah 3:1 we find Satan before God a second time. Zechariah says of his vision, "Then he showed me Joshua the high priest standing before the Angel of the LORD, and Satan standing at his right hand to oppose him" (Zechariah 3:1). Joshua had filthy garments (Zechariah 3:3) and was the priest at the time God was using Zechariah to motivate the Jews to rebuild the temple. "And the LORD said to Satan, 'The LORD rebuke you, Satan! The LORD who has chosen Jerusalem rebuke you! Is this not a brand plucked from the fire?'" (Zechariah 3:2). We aren't given Satan's words, but in some way he was opposing Joshua and God's choosing of Jerusalem.

So then, what does Satan do when he presents himself to God? He accuses and opposes the brethren. John tells us at the midpoint in the Tribulation he heard

> A loud voice saying in heaven, "Now salvation, and strength, and the kingdom of our God, and the power of His Christ have come, for the accuser of our brethren, who accused them before our God day and night, has been cast down."
> *Revelation 12:10*

Satan is accusing all believers before God day and night and will do so until halfway through the Tribulation when he no longer has access to heaven.

Satan splits his time between going before God to accuse the brethren and deceiving the nations on earth while he goes to and fro on it. The only other time we see Satan mentioned in the Old Testament is when "Satan stood up against Israel, and moved David to number Israel" (I Chronicles 21:1). God gave specific instructions in Exodus 30:11-16 that a census was to be accompanied with a ransom for every man to make atonement for everyone so that a plague would not arise. It appears David did not do what God specified, but took a census for other reasons. Therefore, God struck Israel with a plague (I Chronicles 21:7) as Exodus foretold. Satan influenced God's people to sin against Him just as he influenced Adam and Eve in the Garden.

Chapter 4

Satan in the Gospels

The Gospels and the rest of the New Testament mark Satan becoming more active in the world— or at least the New Testament mentions him much more often than the Old Testament. Satan first appears in order to tempt Jesus into sinning (Matthew 4:1-11, Mark 1:12-13, Luke 4:1-13). Did Satan believe he could incite Jesus to sin even though "in Him there is no sin" (1 John 3:5)? Furthermore, since Satan was told by God his head would be bruised (Genesis 3:15), why does he keep fighting against God?

Earlier we talked about Satan's free will and the lack of a salvation plan for him and his fallen angels. Satan cannot change his fate since God already pronounced his judgment. Because of his goal to become like God, it seems Satan's thinking has become so warped that he cannot do anything but rebel against God. Satan will fight against God until he is no longer able even though he cannot win. Does Satan think he still can win and exalt his throne above God? The Bible doesn't give us the answer to this question, but Satan acts as if he thinks he can. Did Satan believe he could tempt Jesus to sin? Again, the Bible doesn't firmly say, but Satan did everything he could to get our Savior to worship him.

During Jesus' testing, Satan reveals a number of details about himself. First, we see Satan's awareness of our physical needs. Satan knew Jesus would be hungry and tried to exploit His bodily need for food (Matthew 4:2-3, Luke 4:2-3). Satan can surely use this same tactic on us; we should be aware of our physical state when we are tempted.

Satan also knows the Scriptures and misinterpreted them in order to tempt Jesus into sinning (Matthew 4:5-6, Luke 4:9-11). Just as he knows our physical weaknesses, Satan knows we can be led astray by a Scripture interpretation that sounds good and appeals to our desires. However Satan's use of Psalm 91:11-12 was taken out of context and was not used "for doctrine, for reproof, for correction, for instruction in righteousness" (II Timothy 3:16); he used it in an attempt to lead Jesus astray just as he twisted God's word in the Garden to deceive Adam and Eve. We must always test any use of Scripture (I Thessalonians 5:21), for Satan is very good at using it for deception.

Jesus defeated all Satan's temptations by using Scripture. As I Thessalonians 5:21 says, testing all things means using Scripture to validate any claim, whether the claim is from the Bible or not. As we become more mature by being filled with wisdom from the Scriptures, we can discern what is right and wrong according to God's truth, not Satan's, thus avoiding deception and sin that comes from being deceived (Hebrews 5:14).

After Satan was unsuccessful in tempting Jesus, "he departed from Him until an opportune time" (Luke 4:13). We will discuss some of the other revelations of Satan's power during Jesus' temptation later, but there are a few more things about Satan's character we learn from this passage.

After showing Jesus the kingdoms of the world, Satan said, "All this authority I will give You, and their glory; for this has been delivered to me, and I give it to whomever I wish" (Luke 4:6). Satan was able to offer Jesus the glory and authority of all the kingdoms of the world because he was the ruler of them. Who delivered their glory and authority to him?

When Adam and Eve were created, God told them, "Be fruitful and multiply; fill the earth and subdue it; have dominion over the fish of the sea, over the birds of the air, and over every living thing that moves on the earth" (Genesis 1:28). When God said to "have dominion," He was giving authority to Adam and Eve to rule over the earth. God's plan was to rule the earth through Adam with Eve at his side. When they sinned, they lost this authority.

We can see mankind's lost authority when God talked to Noah after the flood. God again told the humans who were to populate the earth to "Be fruitful and multiply, and fill the earth" (Genesis 9:1). But instead of telling them to subdue and have dominion over it, He said, "And the fear of you and the dread of you shall be on every beast of the earth, on every bird of the air, on all that move on the earth, and on all the fish of the sea. They are given into your hand" (Genesis 9:2). It sounds similar, but humans no longer have dominion over the earth. Animals are given to us as food and are afraid of humans, but we do not rule over them.

If God is no longer ruling the earth through humans, who has dominion over the earth? God must have delivered this authority to Satan. Jesus even calls Satan the ruler of this world three times in the Gospel of John (John 12:31, 14:30, 16:11). Satan, in turn, can grant authority over kingdoms to whomever he wishes because of his free will. Obviously, Jesus did not accept the offer from Satan and is not yet physically ruling over them. What does this mean for the kingdoms of the world in antiquity and still today?

Satan still has authority over every kingdom of the world.

When we look at kingdoms throughout history, we must realize they, other than Israel who is God's chosen nation, are being directed by Satan because he is the ruler of this world. That does not mean everyone involved in government is evil, unsaved, possessed, or anything like that. However, it does mean government, as an institution, is ruled by Satan. God still has ultimate authority; for example "The king's heart is in the hand of the LORD, like the rivers of water, He turns it wherever He wishes" (Proverbs 21:1). How then does this interaction work between Satan's free will and God's ultimate authority?

There are common phrases about Satan's free will that sound something like, "Satan can only do what God allows him" or, "God has Satan on a leash." However, it seems Satan's free will works the same as ours: we can do essentially whatever we want within the bounds of God's creation, yet God is also completely sovereign over our lives. We see this idea taught in Romans 9:18 where Paul says, "Therefore He has mercy on whom He wills, and whom He wills He hardens," making it sound as if God has total control and we have no free will. Yet, Paul, when speaking about Israel not attaining righteousness, says later in Romans 9:32, "Because they did not seek it by faith, but as it were, by the works of the law," placing the responsibility of believing in Jesus on the Jews which proves our free will. This seems like a contradiction, yet the Bible teaches God's total sovereignty and our total free will.

I believe Satan's free will works the same way. Yes, God has control over Satan because of His will (just like humans), but Satan also has free will to do whatever he wants (just like humans) within the limits of creation. So are the statements such as "God has Satan on a leash" wrong? Not really, but I think it mischaracterizes the interaction between God and Satan's wills. Nobody says, "God had Hitler on a leash," or uses a similar phrase to describe humans' free will; therefore, I think it is good practice to treat Satan's free will the same as ours. Furthermore, we should acknowledge Satan's authority over the kingdoms of the world with a proper respect for how powerful he is while still knowing that God is in control.

There are cases mentioned in the Bible where Satan had to ask God for permission to do something, such as power over all Job had and his flesh (Job 1:11-12, 2:4-6). Interestingly in this case, Satan did not ask for authority over Job but told God to do things to test him which would result in Job cursing God. Instead of taking Satan's bait, God gave Satan power over Job. Satan also asked for Peter to sift him like wheat (Luke 22:31). We already studied how Satan is accusing us before God day and night, but now we learn that at times Satan asks for authority over people to make our faith fail.

In the case of Peter, Jesus didn't directly say whether Satan's request was granted or not, yet He said, "But I have prayed for you, that your faith should not fail" (Luke 22:32). This indicates Satan's request was granted, but what a wonderful thing to know Jesus Himself prayed for Peter to have the strength to withstand Satan's power! Jesus ended His statement by telling Peter, "When you have returned to Me, strengthen your brethren." Peter did deny Jesus three times and this was definitely a failure, but God used his failure to build Peter up into the leader of the Church at Pentecost. Jesus' prayer worked; Peter's faith, although it wavered, did not fail.

God often uses Satan's free will to bring about good. In the lives of both Job and Peter, each man was made better by God giving Satan authority over them. We are never called to defeat Satan, bind him, or anything such thing. We are told stand against him (Ephesians 6:11) and resist him in faith (James 4:7, I Peter 5:9); in doing so, whether he has been granted authority over us or not, he will flee from us (James 4:7) and we will be lifted up (James 4:10). Satan's flight from us may only be for a short time, but we are still given God's promise it will happen. By resisting Satan we are defeating his influence over our lives.

Speaking of Satan's defeat, which we already know is sure, when will he lose authority over the kingdoms of the world? After Jesus' resurrection, He said, "All authority has been given to Me in heaven and on earth" (Matthew 28:18). Paul said of Jesus' work on the cross, "Having disarmed principalities and powers, He made a public spectacle of them, triumphing over them in it" (Colossians 2:15). Satan is part of the "principalities and powers," which means Jesus has already triumphed over him. If this is the case, why don't we see Jesus reigning over the kingdoms of the world now?

In Revelation, a new song is sung:

> You are worthy to take the scroll, and to open its seals;
> For You were slain, and have redeemed us to God by Your blood out of every tribe and tongue and people and nation,
> And have made us kings and priests to our God;
> And we shall reign on the earth.
> *Revelation 5:9-10*

As we said before, Jesus is currently sitting down "at the right hand of God, from that time waiting till His enemies are made His footstool" (Hebrews 10:12-13). Christ will not reign on the earth until He comes back to it. When He comes back in Revelation 19, Satan will be bound and his authority over the earth will be given to Jesus. Jesus will reign over the earth with a woman (the Church) at His side, just as Adam reigned over the earth with Eve at his side. The Bible is amazingly poetic in how God's purpose for creation is realized!

After Jesus' temptation, Satan "departed from Him until an opportune time" (Luke 4:13). Satan appeared next to possess

Judas, which we'll study later. Before that event, Jesus tells us a few things about who Satan is. In Matthew 9:34, the Pharisees say Jesus is casting "out demons by the ruler of the demons." They again make this assertion in Matthew 12:24 except this time they give the ruler of demons the name of Beelzebub/Beelzebul. Jesus does not argue with them about who the ruler of demons is, but instead identifies Beelzebub as Satan (Matthew 12:26). The dragon, or Satan, in Revelation 12:7 is the leader of his angels in the same way Michael is the leader of his angels. From these verses, we know Satan is the ruler over all demons. He must be more powerful than them and there must be some sort of hierarchy Satan has imposed although we aren't told specifically what it is.

We have talked a lot about Satan's deception and in John 8:44 Jesus says he, "does not stand in the truth, because there is no truth in him. When he speaks a lie, he speaks from his own resources, for he is a liar and the father of it." If Satan is anything, he is a liar. He was able to deceive Eve by his craftiness (II Corinthians 11:3) and deceive one third of the angels to follow him (Revelation 12:4). At the time of these deceptions, both Eve and the angels had no sin. Since we have the sin nature through Adam (Romans 5:12) and we know deception will grow worse and worse (II Timothy 3:13), how much more on guard do we need to be against Satan's deception?

Jesus not only called Satan a liar but also a "murderer from the beginning" (John 8:44). Satan not only lies but he also wants to kill. He killed Adam and Eve when he deceived them in the Garden and he is still trying to kill us today. We need to realize how serious the battle with Satan is: he is a liar and a killer.

Chapter 5

Satan in the Church Age

Satan's character is elaborated further in the Epistles. He is very influential in the Church Age, indicating he is more influential now than he was in times past. Paul even calls Satan the "god of this age" in II Corinthians 4:4. If Satan is the god of the current age, then he has enormous influence over those he has blinded, which is why Jesus calls him the "ruler of this world" three times in John. In Ephesians 2:2 Paul calls him the "prince of the power of the air, the spirit who now works in the sons of disobedience." This name may indicate that Satan dwells in the air or the atmosphere of earth (since he cannot dwell in Heaven). Paul warns the Thessalonians the tempter is trying to tempt them away from their faith (I Thessalonians 3:5). He is probably talking about Satan in this passage because there is no human tempter he mentioned in the Epistle. This name of Satan is no surprise because if he tempted Jesus, he will tempt us.

One way Satan tempts us is with sexual enticement. In the city of Thyatira there was a so-called prophetess named Jezebel who was teaching and seducing believers "to commit sexual immorality and eat things sacrificed to idols" (Revelation 2:20).

Those who followed Jezebel along with her doctrine and committed these sins were said to know "the depths of Satan" (Revelation 2:24). In Philadelphia, people who were calling themselves Jews but were not are called "the synagogue of Satan" (Revelation 3:9). Those who are claiming to teach God's truth or to be a part of His family have no part with God but have a strong relationship with Satan whether he is directly involved with their lives or not.

Peter writes to his audience, "Be sober, be vigilant; because your adversary the devil walks about like a roaring lion, seeking whom he may devour" (I Peter 5:8). Satan is certainly our adversary because he accuses us before God (Revelation 12:10). The imagery of a prowling lion is a powerful one; Satan is hunting us to deceive and kill. Additionally, John calls Satan the "wicked one" and the "evil one" in his epistles (I John 2:13-14, 3:12, 5:18-19). There is no end to the depth of Satan's wickedness and evil. We should not underestimate the methods he may use in order to devour us.

In his Epistle, Jude documents a very interesting interaction between Satan and Michael the archangel. He tells us, "Yet Michael the archangel, in contending with the devil, when he disputed about the body of Moses, dared not bring against him a reviling accusation, but said, 'The Lord rebuke you!'" (Jude 9). Of his death, Moses wrote, "So Moses the servant of the LORD died there in the land of Moab, according to the word of the LORD. And He buried him the valley in the land of Moab, opposite Beth Peor; but no one knows his grave to this day" (Deuteronomy 34:5-6). Why did God bury Moses? Why did He give a general location of his grave yet keep the exact spot a secret? When did this happen in relation to Michael and Satan's dispute? And why was Satan disputing about Moses' body in the first place?

The Bible does not give us any answers to these questions, but the only guess I have is that Moses' body would be needed for something after his death. What could be the need? If the two witnesses in Revelation 11:1-14 are Moses and Elijah, they would both need a body while on earth. Elijah never died, but he and his body were taken to heaven (I Kings 2:11). Did God hide Moses' body to be preserved until the Tribulation? Or has Satan contended about other people's bodies, but the Bible does not mention those disputes? Jude writes about this dispute without giving us a lot of answers, so it is good to study it and make speculations while not being dogmatic because we can't know until we get to heaven.

In one of the seven letters to the churches in Revelation, Jesus tells the church at Pergamos Satan dwells in their city and has his throne there (Revelation 2:13). This indicates Satan, although he is splitting his time between heaven and earth, has places he favors being. If Satan dwelt in certain cities back then, it is likely he still does the same thing now. Where could Satan favor being today? London? Washington D.C.? Paris? Moscow? Bejing? Tokyo? Rome? Rio de Janeiro? Jerusalem? Sydney? Ottawa? Cairo? Berlin? We don't know, but what we do know is Christians were still in Pergamos even though Satan was dwelling there. We are called to go and make disciples of all nation (Matthew 28:19). Revelation also tells us that Antipas was a faithful martyr (Revelation 2:13), so make sure God is calling you to go before going to certain places.

Chapter 6

Satan in the Eschaton

The coming of the Antichrist will be "according to the working of Satan, with all power, signs, and lying wonders" (II Thessalonians 2:9). We will study the working and power of Satan in a later section, but there are a few more things to mention about him when talking about his character. In Revelation 12, we are given two signs that summarize Satan and Israel's history on the earth.

First, we see the sign of a woman "clothed with the sun, with the moon under her feet, and on her head a garland of twelve stars" (Revelation 12:1). Who is the identity of this woman? The only other time in Scripture we have a picture of the sun, moon and twelve stars is in Joseph's dream in Genesis 37:9. Jacob understood the meaning of this dream to be Jacob and Joseph's mother as the sun and the moon, and the eleven stars as Joseph's brothers. Who was the twelfth star? Joseph himself. Therefore, when we see the woman clothed as she was in Revelation 12:1, the Bible is talking about the Jewish nation. The woman, or the Jewish nation, "Then being with child, she cried out in labor and in pain to give birth" (Revelation 12:2). Who was the child?

Jesus the Messiah, the One prophesied as the woman's Seed that will bruise Satan's head (Genesis 3:15).

Then the second sign appears: "A great, fiery red dragon having seven heads and ten horns, and seven diadems on his heads" (Revelation 12:3). This dragon, Satan, has multiple heads, horns, and diadems to represent earthly kings and kingdoms he has authority over during the Tribulation which will start as ten kingdoms but three kings will be subdued by the Antichrist (Daniel 7:7-8, 20, 24). The dragon's tail "drew a third of the starts of heaven and threw them to the earth" (Revelation 12:4). The stars in this passage are angels, just like angels were likened to stars in Job 38:7. Angels reside in heaven (Mark 12:25, Luke 2:15), so this must mean Satan was able to deceive one-third on the angels into following him. These angels are now what we call demons or unclean spirits.

"And the dragon stood before the woman who was ready to give birth, to devour her Child as soon as it was born" (Revelation 12:4). The woman, Israel, gave birth to Jesus "who was to rule all nations with a rod of iron" (Revelation 12:5). Satan wants to rule the nations by himself, so naturally he would want to devour this Child. But the Child was "caught up to God and His throne" (Revelation 12:5), meaning that Jesus ascended into Heaven after He completed His work during His first coming.

Now the passage starts taking about what will specifically happen during the Tribulation: "Then the woman fled into the wilderness, where she has a place prepared by God, that they should feed her there one thousand two hundred and sixty days" (Revelation 12:6). One thousand two hundred sixty days is exactly three and a half years according to the Jewish calendar in which years have three hundred sixty days. Therefore, at the midpoint of the Tribulation, Israel will flee into the wilderness and be protected from Satan (Matthew 24:15-28).

Satan in the Eschaton

At this point, a war breaks out in heaven and "Michael and his angels fought with the dragon; and the dragon and his angels fought" (Revelation 12:7). What exactly prompts this war at this point? Maybe God tells Satan he no longer can ask for authority over people and Satan threw a fit and started the war? Maybe Satan decided he would fight in heaven instead of earth? We don't know, but we do know Satan and his angels, "did not prevail, nor was place found for them in heaven any longer" (Revelation 12:8).

Satan "was cast to the earth, and his angels were cast out with him" (Revelation 12:9). For the second half of the Tribulation, Satan and his angels no longer have access to heaven and Satan cannot accuse the brethren before God's throne. Satan now has a lot more time to spend on earth to work toward his goal of ascending his throne above God's. He uses this time to persecute "the woman who gave birth to the male child. But the woman was given two wings of a great eagle, that she might fly into the wilderness to her place, where she is nourished for a time and times and half a time, from the presence of the serpent" (Revelation 12:13-14). God supernaturally protects Israel from Satan by creating her escape and sustaining her in the wilderness.

Satan tries to stop Israel's escape by spewing "water out of his mouth like a flood after the woman, that he might cause her to be carried away by the flood" (Revelation 12:15). John can use water and the sea to represent Gentile nations in the book of Revelation (Revelation 17:15), and the "flood" in this passage probably symbolizes the Gentile nations. Satan will use the armies and weapons of the Gentiles to try to kill Israel. "But the earth helped the woman, and the earth opened its mouth and swallowed up the flood which the dragon had spewed out of his mouth" (Revelation 12:16). God will protect Israel by creating a hole in the earth and swallowing up the Gentile armies sent after

Israel during her flight to the wilderness.

"And the dragon was enraged with the woman, and he went to make war with the rest of her offspring, who keep the commandments of God and have the testimony of Jesus Christ" (Revelation 12:17). God's protection of Israel causes Satan to turn his attention away from Israel and put his focus on believers among all the other nations.

This will be a terrible time for humans left on earth. The Bible even says, "Woe to the inhabitants of the earth and the sea! For the devil has come down to you, having great wrath, because he knows that he has a short time" (Revelation 12:12). God's wrath is being poured out on the earth during the Tribulation, and for the second half Satan focuses his full attention and wrath on those left on the earth. Lying and murdering — which is what Satan does — will be extremely intense during this period. These two great wraths will culminate in Satan and his armies marching to Megiddo/Armageddon, the final battle before Jesus' return (Revelation 16:16).

Satan and Jesus' armies meet in battle, but it does not seem like much of a fight. There is no description of what the battle is like. Simply, the beast and the false prophet are captured, and "cast alive into the lake of fire burning with brimstone. And the rest were killed with the sword which proceeded from the mouth of Him who sat on the horse" (Revelation 19:20-21). It sounds as if Jesus plucks the beast and false prophet from their place in the army and then the rest of the army is destroyed at Jesus' word. Not much of a battle when God is fighting!

Satan is then bound in the bottomless pit and sealed for a thousand years while Jesus reigns on the earth (Revelation 20:2-3). "Now when the thousand years have expired, Satan will be released from his prison and will go out to deceive the nations which are in the four corners of the earth, Gog and Magog, to gather them together to battle, whose number is as the sand of the sea" (Revelation 20:7-8). How sinful is man that even when Jesus is physically reigning on the earth they would rather follow Satan when he appears than believe in Jesus for deliverance from the same fate as the Antichrist and false prophet. We can assume people at the beginning of the Tribulation will tell their children about what happened in the battle of Armageddon (Jeremiah 23:7-8). What will happen in the Millennium that will make so many people susceptible to Satan's deception? We don't know exactly, but we do know, "The heart is deceitful above all things, and desperately wicked; who can know it?" (Jeremiah 17:9). Man's inclination toward sin is so strong that his pride will cause so many to not believe in Jesus even when the conditions on earth are near perfect (Isaiah 65:20-25).

Satan will deceive people into believing they can defeat Jesus this time even though the last battle was a failure. This is Satan's last attempt to ascend his throne above God's. Satan's army will go up on the breadth of the earth and surround "the camp of the saints and the beloved city" (Revelation 20:9). They are prepared for battle, but again it will not be much of a fight. "And the fire came down from God out of heaven and devoured them" (Revelation 20:9). The final verse in the Bible mentioning Satan says, "The devil, who deceived them, was cast into the lake of fire and brimstone where the beast and the false prophet are. And they will be tormented day and night forever and ever" (Revelation 20:10). Satan's ultimate end is in the lake of fire with the Antichrist and false prophet. This "unholy trinity" will be tormented forever for everything they have done. Since we know this is the result of the devil, should we not want to follow God instead of Satan's deception?

SATAN'S POWER

In the previous section, we studied Satan's character and motivations from his creation to ultimate judgment. Now we will look at his power and works which are all focused on deceiving us into not following our Creator and worshiping him instead. As we talk about Satan's power, anything he was able to do in the past he is certainly able to do today and as we get closer to the Tribulation we should see more displays of his power in the world. However, Satan is not the cause of every disease or natural disaster. It is a possibility, but we should not immediately assume Satan is directly involved. There are many causes for negative events, not the least of which is our personal sin and God's judgment. Of all the bad things that happen in the Bible, it is rare the Scriptures attribute these events to Satan's direct intervention. We should take the same approach as we study Satan's power; while he is capable of many signs, we should never assume Satan is the cause unless it is obvious he is.

One power Satan is never mentioned as having is the power to create. Yet some of Satan's powers, such as the power to inflict disease (Job 2:7) or make fire come from heaven (Job 1:16), may imply he has a limited ability to create things. If he can create things, is that why he thought he could be like the Most High (Isaiah 14:14)? It is hard to know whether this is true or not, but even if Satan does have the ability to create, God's power in all cases is superior. None of Satan's powers are even comparable to God's ability which is able to protect us completely (Romans 8:37-39).

Chapter 7

Satan's Power in the Garden

Although this book is primarily about signs and wonders, it would be a mistake to not to talk about Satan's intellect as a big part of his power to deceive. In the Garden of Eden, Satan's deception was primarily conversation and leading Eve down a mental path eventually culminating in her sinning.

> Now the serpent was more cunning than any beast of the field which the LORD God had made. And he said to the woman, "Has God indeed said, 'You shall not eat of every tree in the garden'?" And the woman said to the serpent, "We may eat the fruit of the trees of the garden; but of the fruit of the tree which is in the midst of the garden, God has said, 'You shall not eat it, nor shall you touch it, lest you die.'" Then the serpent said to the woman, "You will not surely die. For God knows that in the day you eat of it your eyes will be opened, and you will be like God, knowing good and evil."
> *Genesis 3:1-5*

Deceiving by Signs

 First, Satan questioned God's Word seemingly innocently (Genesis 3:1). However, he asked it in a way that mischaracterized what God said. God commanded Adam to not eat from only one tree while giving every other tree as food (Genesis 2:16-17). But the way Satan asked his question made it sound as if God did not allow Adam and Even to eat from any tree of the garden. Satan will not ask, "What did God say?" but rather he'll ask his question in a way that puts doubt into our heart or starts us down a path Satan has already anticipated; a path which ends in us sinning.

 After Eve's answer, which was not quite correct with her mentioning she was not allowed to touch the tree (Genesis 3:3), Satan lied and directly contradicted God's Word (Genesis 3:4). His first question seemed innocent enough, but it got Eve into a conversation with him. It is very likely Satan already had responses planned for what Eve might say. If Satan stopped talking after his direct lie, Eve might have been able to handle Satan's deception because it was so obviously false. However, he didn't stop the conversation.

 Next, he gave Eve a reason why God gave the command. Satan will often impose a motive on God's commands to make it sound as if He is keeping us from fun or arbitrarily making rules because He's a mean God. When Satan said God knew her eyes would be opened and she would know the difference between good and evil when she at the fruit (Genesis 3:5), this was actually true. However, God's motives are are always in our best interest to keep us from sin and death.

 Satan did not tell Eve God was looking out for her and Adam to keep them from death. Instead, he made it sound as if God was keeping them from being like Him by saying, "You will be like God" (Genesis 3:5). This was a lie and also exactly what Satan wanted (Isaiah 14:13-14); he used the same desire that corrupted him to deceive Eve. Who wouldn't want the power to create a universe? Who wouldn't want to rule over their creation with total authority and power? Eve fell to the same desire as Satan, ate the fruit, and Adam ate as well.

II Corinthians 11:3 says, "The serpent deceived Eve by his craftiness." Satan asked a question which started a conversation. Then he used a lie and the truth together to prompt a desire within Eve to get her to sin. Throughout the rest of the Bible, as far as Satan's craftiness is concerned, Satan does not deviate from this pattern. He asks a question to put us on the defensive or get us to doubt what we know about God's Word. Then he uses a mixture of lies, truths, and appeals to our desires to get us to turn away from God's Word. Any conversation with Satan that is allowed to progress will bring us closer to sinning. As a model of defense, when Satan tried to start conversations with Jesus during His temptation, in each case Jesus quoted God's Word, and the conversation was over. Even when statements in a conversation may not be obvious contradictions of Scripture, we should be constantly evaluating every question or answer by God's Word and be careful about where those statements may be leading the dialogue.

We could study at length all the different ways Satan uses lies, truths, and appeals to desire, but that would be outside the scope of this book. But we should always remember Satan uses his intellect along with his signs to deceive us. Ultimately, any sign can be interpreted in more than one way. Therefore, the Bible must always be our guide when interpreting the source and reason for a sign so that our minds will not be corrupted "from the simplicity that is in Christ" (II Corinthians 11:3).

Satan did use a sign in the Garden, although its not a sign we would typically recognize. Satan did not appear to Eve as a cherub. He appears as a serpent, an animal which Eve likely had seen. The Bible relates the serpent to the beasts of the field twice in Genesis 3:1 and 3:14. When God curses the serpent, He says the serpent will go on his belly and shall eat dust all the days of his life (Genesis 3:14). If God said the serpent would go on his belly, that indicates serpents were not on their belly before the curse. Apparently, serpents will also eat dust during the Millennium when God restores much of the earth to pre-fall conditions (Isaiah 65:25, Micah 7:17).

So what exactly appeared to Eve? We know Satan is a cherub, not an actual serpent. If Satan only took the form of a serpent, it seems odd for God to relate it to the beasts of the field twice and curse the animal for the rest of earth's existence. Does that mean Satan possessed a serpent and used that animal to talk with Eve? Demons can possess animals (Luke 8:33) so theoretically Satan can too. Which way did it happen? The form of a serpent or possessing of a serpent? The Bible doesn't give us a clear answer, but it seems some interaction between Satan and at least one serpent occurred in order for both Satan and the animal to be cursed.

The animal Eve talked to in the Garden must have been what we now call a snake. Before the Fall, it had legs, but God removed their legs one way or another. Snakes are the only animal "on its belly," and because of how close its head is to the ground, it does "eat dust" (Isaiah 65:25). Micah 7:17 uses the same Hebrew word for "serpent" as well as another word that can be translated "snake:" "They shall lick the dust like a serpent; they shall crawl from their holes like snakes of the earth." This part of the verse is Hebrew parallelism, which indicates serpent and snake are the same creature.

Not only does the Biblical evidence point to a snake being the animal that deceived Eve, but in pagan religions snakes often appear as prominent animals: the Egyptians had stories of their gods that included snakes, the Greek god Apollo used a serpent as his symbol, the Serpent Mound was built by the inhabitants of what is now Ohio, and many other examples. It is outside the scope of this book to study the serpent in religions across the world, but Satan seems to still favor the snake to represent himself.

So what do we make of the serpent in relation to Satan's power? Either Satan has the power to influence and even possess animals or he can appear in the form of an animal or both. Can he appear as other animals or combinations of animals? In many ancient religions there are stories of chimeras, creatures made up of body parts of different animals. Examples would include Egyptian gods having the body of a human but the head of an animal or the chimera, where the term to describe these animals came from, that had the body and head of a lion, the tail of a snake, and the head of a goat coming out of its back.

Were these creatures based on something or imagined by the people of the time? Probably a little of both. If Satan has the ability to appear as an animal, he could possibly appear as a combination of animals. Satan has the ability to create visions for people, which we'll study in his testing of Jesus, and could give people visions of strange creatures. Once a person got ideas of combining different parts of animals, their imagination could work from there and create new ones. Or it is possible these creatures were all made up and written into stories like any modern author would do.

While Satan's intervention in these stories is not provable, in some way he has power to use and/or imitate animals. Above all, the last thing we would want to do is communicate and take direction from a talking snake because we know how that turned out last time!

Chapter 8

Satan's Power of Influence

Whenever we sin, we are "of the devil, for the devil has sinned from the beginning" (I John 3:8). This goes for believers and non-believers; all sin is of the devil. All believers sin because we retain the sin nature (Roman 7:13-25, Colossians 3:9-10). Once God gives us eternal life by believing in Jesus we are secure in our salvation because we have passed from death to life and cannot pass back into death because Jesus is faithful (John 5:24, II Timothy 2:13). But when we sin, "In this the children of God and the children of the devil are manifest: whoever does not practice righteousness is not of God, nor is he who does not love his brother" (I John 3:10). When someone practices unrighteousness, whether they are saved or not, they are of the devil and children of the devil.

Does that mean a saved person can be "of the devil?" It certainly does, but it does not mean a saved person can become unsaved or was never saved. It means we are acting like our old sin nature. Where did the sin nature come from? Adam's original sin in the Garden (Romans 5:12). And this sin descended from Satan (Ezekiel 28:15-16). Therefore, when we sin, we are of the devil because we are following his works of rebellion against God.

The earliest person said to be "of the devil" was Cain. Cain "was of the wicked one and murdered his brother. And why did he murder him? Because his works were evil and his brother's righteous" (I John 3:12). Cain followed Satan's way of sin and committed murder which made him of the wicked one. We could even call Cain one of Satan's children. When the Bible talks about the sons of the devil (John 8:44), it means they are so strongly influenced by Satan that they carry out his desires. Satan puts his children among believers (Matthew 13:38-39) which can increase his influence in a believer's life.

Lying is of the evil one because Jesus said, "But let your 'Yes' be 'Yes,' and your 'No,' 'No.' For whatever is more than these is from the evil one" (Matthew 5:37). We also see Satan and lying connected in the story on Ananias and Sapphira. As a side note, this couple must have been saved because the Apostles would not have allowed unsaved people into the fellowship of the Church this early in it's existence. However, both of them lied about how much money they were giving to the Church. Peter said to Ananias, "Ananias, why has Satan filled your heart to lie to the Holy Spirit and keep back part of the price of the land for yourself?" (Acts 5:3). Peter did not mean Ananias was possessed by Satan in his heart, but lies, which are of the devil (John 8:44), were his actions. Did Satan have a direct influence on Ananias and Sapphira? We aren't told, but we do know whenever we lie we are acting like the devil.

The extent of Satan's power to influence people is given to us in I John 5:19: "The whole world lies under the sway of the wicked one." Paul calls the devil the "god of this age" and his influence can be so strong over non-believers that he can blind men's minds to the Gospel (II Corinthians 4:3-4) and even snatch it away (Matthew 13:19, Mark 4:15, Luke 8:12). Believers can even turn aside after Satan and stop following God's commands (I Timothy 5:15).

In some cases, the sin of believers is so bad they are delivered "to Satan for the destruction of the flesh" (I Corinthians 5:5). The man in this instance was having a sexual relationship with his father's wife (I Corinthians 5:1). Notice only his flesh/body is delivered to Satan, but his spirit is "saved in the day of the Lord Jesus (I Corinthians 5:5). This means if a believer is delivered to Satan because of his sin, the devil will afflict him but he is still going to heaven.

Another example of believers being delivered to Satan are Hymenaeus and Alexander. Paul delivered them "to Satan that they may learn not to blaspheme" (I Timothy 1:20). But Paul also describes these two as rejecting faith and a good conscience, so their blaspheming was an outward working of the rejection that already took place (I Timothy 1:19). The consequences for Hymenaeus and Alexander are left ambiguous, but given the example of the man from Corinth, their affliction was probably a physical ailment.

Satan's influence over the world is very strong and will only grow stronger as we move closer to the Tribulation. Thankfully, God gives us the tools to stand against his deception which we will spend an entire chapter on later in this book.

Chapter 9

Satan's Power over Job

After Satan went out from the presence of the LORD in Job 1:12, an account is given of what happened: Job's oxen and servants were killed by a band of Sabeans, his sheep and servants were killed by the fire of God, Chaldeans stole his camels and killed his servants, and a great wind killed all his children (Job 1:13-19). These things happened because God gave everything Job had into Satan's power (Job 1:12).

Satan must have the power to persuade people to act in certain ways, which would explain the Sabeans and the Chaldeans' actions against Job. How exactly did he do it? We are not told, but Satan could have used the same tactics he used with Eve in addition to any of the other powers we will discuss. Satan was also able to move "David to number Israel" (I Chronicles 21:1). We also know Cain "was of the wicked one" (I John 3:12). Humans are very susceptible to Satan's power of influence if we are not guarded properly against it.

Not only could Satan use his power to incite people to act against Job, but he was also able to make fire come down from the sky. The messenger to Job called it the fire of God, but it was actually the fire of Satan. Satan being able to bring down fire from heaven will appear again with the false prophet during the Tribulation (Revelation 13:13). In Job, the purpose of this fire is to kill, but in Revelation the purpose is to deceive although it might kill as well.

The next display of Satan's power in Job was a great wind, probably a tornado. This great wind was powerful enough to knock down the house where Job's children were eating and drinking and killed them all. Satan, then, has power over the forces of nature at least to some extent.

After Satan met with God again, He gave Satan power over Job's body but was not allowed to kill him (Job 2:6). Satan "struck Job with painful boils from the sole of his foot to the crown of his head" (Job 2:7). Satan has the power to inflict physical ailments, a power which we will see again in the Gospels.

What do all of these things teach us? When Satan is given permission by God, he has enormous power over people's actions, disease, and nature even to the point of killing people. Does Satan in his free will always have the ability to perform these signs or must he always ask for permission? The Bible doesn't answer this question, but practically speaking it doesn't matter whether we know the answer. We will never know who Satan is accusing or over whom God gives him authority. We should always be aware of Satan's enormous power over people especially as we move ever closer to the Tribulation.

Chapter 10

Satan's Power in the Gospels

In the temptation of Jesus, the next time in the Bible we see Satan's power displayed, Satan was able to bring Jesus to two different locations: Jerusalem and an exceedingly high mountain (Matthew 4:5, 8, Luke 4:5, 9). Matthew says he "took" Jesus to both places and Luke says he "took" Him on the mountain and "brought" Him to Jerusalem. After Satan left Jesus, angels ministered to Him (Matthew 4:11) and He returned in the power of the Spirit to Galilee (Luke 4:14). Did Satan return Jesus to the wilderness after bringing him to the mountain and Jerusalem? Does this mean Satan is able to physically transport human bodies to different locations very quickly? Or did he only show Jesus visions?

In the case of Satan taking Jesus to Jerusalem, they had to actually be there because Satan tells Jesus to throw Himself down from the top of the temple (Matthew 4:6, Luke 4:9). This would make little sense if it was only a vision. Matthew and Luke also used the verbs "took" and "brought" indicating a change in location. If it was only a vision, they could have used a phrase such as "showed Him the temple" like they did when Satan

57

"showed Him all the kingdoms of the world" (Luke 4:5). These passages strongly indicate Satan can transport humans to different locations throughout the world very quickly.

Speaking of Satan showing Jesus the kingdoms of the world, there is no single mountain in which to view every kingdom, but Matthew does say it is "exceedingly high" (Matthew 4:8). Furthermore, Satan "showed Him all the kingdoms of the world in a moment of time" (Luke 4:5) and "their glory" (Matthew 4:8). How did Satan do all this? If he transported Jesus to one location at Jerusalem, then, to be consistent, Satan only transported Jesus to one mountain. The passage doesn't indicated Satan took Jesus around the world to see every kingdom, but only show them to Him. Does this mean Satan is able to show people visions? I believe this is the indication of the Scripture. If these two things are true, that Satan can transport us and show us visions, these are two very powerful tools Satan can use to deceive us.

In a speculation beyond the text, if the mountain was "exceedingly high" (Matthew 4:8), the atmospheric conditions may have been difficult for a human to survive. If that is the case, Satan may be able to protect our bodies from harmful things in the opposite way he inflicts disease on people. This is speculation, but I am offering it here as another possible power of Satan.

Satan's power is mentioned by Jesus when He encountered "a woman who had a spirit of infirmity eighteen years, and was bent over and could in no way raise herself up" (Luke 13:11). Jesus heals her, and after being corrected by the ruler of the synagogue not to heal on the Sabbath, He responded, "So ought not this woman, being a daughter of Abraham, whom Satan has bound—think of it—for eighteen years, be loosed from this bond on the Sabbath?" (Luke 13:16). Satan must have the power to inflict physical damage on our bodies resulting in muscular and skeletal infirmities.

Peter says in Acts that, "God anointed Jesus of Nazareth with the Holy Spirit and with power, who went about doing good and healing all who were oppressed by the devil, for God was with Him" (Acts 10:38). While this verse does not tell us how many were oppressed by the devil as opposed to those suffering from ailments as a consequence of living in a sinful world, it indicates that of the healings Jesus performed enough of the infirmities were from the oppression of the devil for Peter to make mention here.

Satan and his spirits were afflicting many people during the ministry of Christ (we will discuss how demons afflicted people in another chapter). Outside of a few references in other books of the Bible, we do not see this concentration of Satan's direct intervention in people's lives other times in history. But it is possible that if Satan was very active surrounding Jesus' first coming, he will be very active again at His second coming. As we see a rise in his deception by signs, we could also see a rise in disease and other bodily ailments as we come closer to Jesus' return. As stated in the beginning of this section on Satan's power, we don't want to attribute every sickness to Satan's direct intervention, but it is a possibility of which to be aware.

During the last year of Jesus' earthly life as the Feast of Unleavened Bread was drawing near, "Satan entered Judas... So he went his way and conferred with the chief priests and captains, how he might betray Him to them" (Luke 22:3, 4). Satan is capable of possessing humans although Judas is the only direct reference of him doing so. Judas was never a believer (John 6:64) and he was already in contention with what Jesus was doing. Judas had gotten angry about Mary anointing Jesus' feet with expensive spikenard, not because he cared about using the money for the poor but because he was a thief (John 12:3-6).

Deceiving by Signs

A few days later, Jesus was anointed again, this time on his head (Mark 14:3). His disciples were angry and even criticized the woman for using the expensive oil (Mark 14:4-5). Judas must have been included in this group of disciples. Satan entered Judas' body, apparently influencing him to go to the chief priests and work out a way to betray Jesus (Mark 14:10-11).

Satan must have left Judas' body because during the last supper, Satan entered Judas again after Jesus identified him as the betrayer (John 13:27). We aren't told how long Satan stayed in Judas, but we can at least assume he stayed long enough for Judas to betray him just as Satan influenced him to make the deal with the chief priests. Satan may have left him after the betrayal was complete because Judas felt remorse for his actions, although he still never placed his faith in Jesus and then committed suicide (Matthew 27:3-5). We do know Judas received a very bad punishment in hell after his death (Mark 14:21), so "the devil didn't make him do it" so to speak even though having Satan possessing him must have been a very strong evil influence.

We aren't given any information on the circumstances for why Satan was allowed or was able to enter Judas. The case will be made in the later chapter on demon possession that there must be some act on a human's part for a demon to enter them. We aren't told of any such action on Judas' part, but only that he was displeased with Jesus' actions (John 12:3-6, Mark 14:4-5). Satan's ability to possess a human may be based on different factors, but the Bible doesn't give us any information on what they might be. Lest anyone be concerned about someone being possessed by Satan, there is only one other person in all of history mentioned in Scripture that Satan may possess.

Judas is called the son of perdition in John 17:12 and the Antichrist is also called the son of perdition in II Thessalonians 2:3. Given this similarity as well as the proximity of both men to Jesus' first and second coming respectively as well as the many references in the Bible to Satan giving the Antichrist power, it is possible that Satan will possess the Antichrist too. The Bible does not say this directly, but it is very likely to be the case.

One more observation about Satan possessing Judas is the proximity to Jesus in which Satan carried out the possession. Jesus and Judas were literally face to face when Satan possessed him and Jesus may have even been talking to Satan instead of Judas when He said, "What you do, do quickly" (John 13:27). From this we should learn that Satan can influence people no matter where they are, even if they are in a church service or setting.

Chapter 11

Satan's Power in the Church Age

Satan's power during the Church Age seems to be largely focused on stopping the spread of the Gospel and hindering the Church's actions. This makes sense because the dispensations of the Church and the law are so different. In the age of the law, Satan is only mentioned a few times and his focus is causing Israel to sin in order to break their covenant with God, ultimately stopping the Messiah from coming. During the Church age, God is using the Church to spread the Good News of Jesus' death and resurrection to all nations rather than focusing specifically on the nation of Israel. Therefore it makes sense Satan would want to stop this spread instead of trying to get Israel to sin.

The spread of the Gospel can be stopped in two ways: obstructing people's ability to believe in Jesus and stopping believers from talking about Him. During Paul's defense to King Agrippa, he talked about the purpose for which Jesus appeared to him: "I will deliver you from the Jewish people, as well as from the Gentiles, to whom I now send you, to open their eyes, in order to turn them from darkness to light, and from the power of

Satan to God, that they may receive forgiveness of sins and an inheritance among those who are sanctified by faith in Me" (Acts 26:17-18). Paul reveals Satan's power is focused on "closing people's eyes" to the Gospel so that they would not receive forgiveness of sins and an inheritance by faith.

Paul says in II Timothy 2:24-26, "And a servant of the Lord must not quarrel but be gentle to all, able to teach, patient, in humility correcting those who are in opposition, if God perhaps will grant them repentance, so that they may know the truth, and that they may come to their senses and escape the snare of the devil, having been taken captive by him to do his will." The Greek word translated "taken captive" is the same word translated "catch" when Jesus said to Simon Peter, "From now on you will catch men" (Luke 5:10). The word means "to take as a prisoner of war." Satan's goal is to get people in a trap they cannot escape to carry out his will.

II Timothy 2:24-26 is very likely talking about believers being trapped because Paul is instructing Timothy about how to act among believers and charge those in the faith (II Timothy 2:14-18). Obviously unbelievers can be taken captive by Satan as Acts 26:17-18 pointed out by blinding them to the light of the Gospel (II Corinthians 4:4), but believers can be trapped as well. They are still saved, but can become Satan's captive to do what he wants. Believers should be well aware Satan can use Christians to accomplish his purposes. When we notice someone in the Church not carrying out God's will, we should not assume they are unsaved or accuse them of being "of the devil." Rather, we should do what God said, to not quarrel, be gentle, and in humility correcting them (II Timothy 2:24-25). As we study Satan's power in our current age, we should remember any distraction from believing or communicating the Gospel fulfills Satan's goal.

After Paul founded the Corinthian church, they asked him a question about a man's touching of a woman (I Corinthians 7:1). Paul teaches them about the intimate relationship between a husband and wife and says, "Do not deprive one another except with consent for a time, that you may give yourselves to fasting and prayer; and come together again so that Satan does not tempt you because of your lack of self-control" (I Corinthians 7:5). Satan will use unmet sexual desires of the husband or wife to tempt the couple. If a husband or wife lacks self-control, Satan can exploit their focus on filling their desire instead of prayer or whatever else God called them to do.

Paul mentions Satan's influence again in his second letter to the Corinthians when talking about forgiveness. He says, "Now whom you forgive anything, I also forgive. For if indeed I have forgiven anything, I have forgiven that one for your sakes in the presence of Christ, lest Satan should take advantage of us; for we are not ignorant of his devices" (II Corinthians 2:10-11). If we do not forgive people, Satan can take advantage of us. The lack of forgiveness of a man in the Corinthian church was causing trouble because Paul did not want him to be "swallowed up with too much sorrow" (II Corinthians 2:7). This not only hurts the man who was punished, but is actually disobedient to God to not forgive (II Corinthians 2:9).

If we are disobedient in one thing, Satan can tempt us into being disobedient in other things. Paul tells the Ephesians to not, "give place to the devil" (Ephesians 4:27). Any "place" we give Satan affords him the opportunity to tempt us into more sin.

In II Corinthians 6:14-15, Paul says, "Do not be unequally yoked together with unbelievers. For what fellowship has righteousness with lawlessness? And what communion has light with darkness? And what accord has Christ with Belial? Or what part has a believer with an unbeliever?" Belial is another way to talk about Satan, and Jesus has no accord with him. There is no positive relationship between the two, and Paul uses this picture to describe our relationship with unbelievers. An improper relationship with an unbeliever can cause filthiness of the flesh and spirit (II Corinthians 7:1).

It is worth noting this passage is talking about being unequally yoked with unbelievers, but it is not saying we do not associate those who do not believe. Jesus associated with many unbelievers, even going to their house for meals. But He was never yoked or engaged in a very close relationship with them. We should be very careful with whom we associate and grow close because an improper relationship would be the same as Jesus having fellowship with Satan.

Paul tells us Satan hindered him from traveling back to the Thessalonians more than once (I Thessalonians 2:18). We don't know the circumstances, but we learn Satan has the power, probably through influencing humans, to prevent people from going to certain locations. We also know the Holy Spirit forbid Paul from traveling to Asia (Acts 16:6). How did Paul discern who was preventing his travels? My guess is either God told him or it was very obvious it was Satan or God. If we are hindered from travel, we can always trust God that He knows exactly where He wants us at all times.

Hebrews 2:14-15 says, "Inasmuch then as the children have partaken of flesh and blood, He Himself likewise shared in the same, that through death He might destroy him who had the power of death, that is, the devil, and release those who through fear of death were all their lifetime subject to bondage." Satan has power over death because his deception influenced Adam and Eve to sin which brought death into the world. People will often fall to Satan's deception because of their fear of dying. If they do not know what comes after they die or think earthly life is all they have, it is very easy to hold onto this life and its pleasures, not realizing the consequences Satan's deception will bring.

But Jesus, by His death and resurrection, gives us eternal life, thus destroying the power and fear death held over us. In contrast with unbelievers, believers should understand our earthly life is temporary and life if heaven will be far better (Philippians 1:23). This should largely marginalize and hopefully eradicate our fear of dying, even if we still do not look forward to a painful death or leaving our loved ones behind. Without the fear of death and going to hell, one of Satan's most powerful weapons has be taken away. By His death and resurrection, Jesus destroyed Satan because He restored humanity to a deathless existence. How thankful we should be that Satan and his power was completely destroyed at the cross!

Chapter 12

Satan's Power in the Eschaton

Satan is working hard to bring about his rule of the world that will ultimately be manifested in the Antichrist's reign. John tells us, "It is the last hour; and as you have heard that the Antichrist is coming, even now many antichrists have come, by which we know that it is the last hour" (I John 2:18). Satan's focus during the church age is to blind people from believing the Gospel and hinder Christians from spreading it, but he is also effecting world events in order to shift the kingdoms of the earth to a old world government. The spirit of the Antichrist, which is Satan using humans to obtain a one world government that will worship him, "is now already in the world" (I John 4:3). If John saw the spirit of the Antichrist in his day, how much closer are we to his rule after two thousand years!

Paul calls the spirit of the Antichrist the mystery of lawlessness in II Thessalonians 2:7-8, saying, "For the mystery of lawlessness is already at work; only He who now restrains will do so until He is taken out of the way. And then the lawless one will be revealed." The only thing holding back the Antichrist from ruling is "He who now restrains," which I believe is the

Holy Spirit through the Church. At the Rapture, the Church will be removed from the earth which takes away the medium through which the Holy Spirits restrains. The Holy Spirit will still be here because people will still get saved during the Tribulation, but His restraining influence over the Antichrist will disappear. Once the Church is gone, Satan will have no opposition, except infighting within his ranks, to bring the Antichrist to power.

"The coming of the lawless one is according to the working of Satan, with all power, signs, and lying wonders, and with all unrighteous deception among those who perish, because they did not receive the love of the truth, that they might be saved" (II Thessalonians 2:9-10). This means events that move the nations closer to a one world government ruled by the lawless one are the working of Satan. When we see lies being told about world events or lying wonders, we should realize Satan is ultimately responsible.

Those who tell lies or believe them do not love truth (II Thessalonians 2:10), "And for this reason God will send them strong delusion, that they should believe the lie, that they all may be condemned who did not believe the truth but had pleasure in unrighteousness" (II Thessalonians 2:11-12). These people not only did not love the truth but they enjoyed being unrighteous. The delusion God will send, at least in part, must be the increased power and influence Satan and his demons will have during the Tribulation as well as the Antichrist (the first seal in Revelation 6:1-2) and the false prophet. Furthermore, "Many will come in My name, saying, 'I am the Christ,' and will deceive many. And you will hear of wars and rumors of wars... Then many false prophets will rise up and deceive many" (Matthew 24:5-6, 11).

Satan's biggest deception is his claim to be the savior of the world. In order to be a savior, there has to be a problem from

Satan's Power in the Eschaton

which to be delivered. In our time and more so as history continues, Satan is creating an enormous amount of chaos because eventually the Antichrist will appear and claim to be able to solve all the world's problems. Yet, through the chaos Satan still promises "peace and safety" (I Thessalonians 5:3).

In John's vision he "looked, and behold, a white horse. He who sat on it had a bow; and a crown was given to him, and he went out conquering and to conquer" (Revelation 6:2). The Antichrist will appear as a savior on a white horse just like Jesus will appear on a white horse at the end of the Tribulation (Revelation 19:11). What will the Antichrist go out to conquer? Not sin and the solution to humanity's depravity, but all the problems in the world Satan created to bring him into power. The solutions to the problems will actually be very bad for people, causing a lot of death (for example Revelation 6:8) and strict control over their lives (for example Revelation 13:16-17). Satan will use unbelievers' fear of death (Hebrews 2:15) and other deceptions to deceive them into thinking the Antichrist's solutions will end the chaos. Eventually Antichrist will be given authority "over every tribe, tongue, and nation" (Revelation 13:7). How deceptive that Satan is able to create a problem and then offer a solution that leaves humanity in a worse position than it started with most people never realizing what happened to them.

When the lawless one, the Antichrist, comes he will accept Satan's offer that Jesus rejected. In Revelation 13:2 it says, "The dragon gave him his power, his throne, and great authority." This means Satan, in one way or another, offered the Antichrist all the authority of the kingdoms of the world and their glory (Luke 4:6) and he accepted it. Satan will also grant power to the false prophet who will play a large role in forcing people to worship Antichrist and Satan (Revelation 13:12-15).

During the Tribulation, the Antichrist will even be mortally wounded and then healed (Revelation 13:3). Who will heal him? The next verse says, "So they worshiped the dragon who gave authority to the beast; and they worshiped the beast, saying, 'Who is like the beast? Who is able to make war with him?" (Revelation 13:4). The world will know Satan healed the beast and in turn worship both him and the Antichrist. Will the Antichrist be dead and then resurrected or is this event a part of Satan's deception and the death is faked? Depending on how you read Revelation 13:2 and 13:12, I think it could possibly be either one. Nevertheless, the world will believe he was dead and raised back to life by Satan. In this Satan will mimic Jesus' resurrection with his own counterfeit messiah and receive the worship he has always desired.

So far in this chapter, we have focused on the "unrighteous deception" part of the "coming of the lawless one" in II Thessalonians 2:9-10. Yet equally important are the "power, signs, and lying wonders" Satan will use to bring the Antichrist into power. The signs will most likely be all the powers we have discussed in this chapter but done to a greater magnitude such that they might seem like a new kind of sign. In a later section, will address signs we see today that are part of the mystery of lawlessness, but this will be conjecture. God has given us the information we need to not be "shaken in mind or troubled, either by spirit or by word or by letter" (II Thessalonians 2:2). We will not be deceived if we hold fast to Scripture and test everything (I Thessalonians 5:21).

Chapter 13

Our Defense Against Satan's Power

The world is gradually growing closer to Satan's peak of power and influence. We have already seen Satan's defeat when Jesus appears, then once and for all at the end of the Millennium. In the meantime, how are we to defend ourselves against Satan's deception and power? Thankfully, there are many ways God protects us, but His protection against Satan is not automatic. We must appropriate each defense God gives us in the proper way to stand against the wiles of the devil.

Prayer is one of the strongest defenses against Satan. Jesus told us very specifically to pray, "Do not lead us into temptation, but deliver us from the evil one" (Matthew 6:13). Praying for deliverance from Satan should be part of our prayer routine which should constantly remind us that we need this protection. Not only do we pray for protection for ourselves, but Jesus prayed for us as well. He prayed for God to keep the eleven disciples from the evil one (John 17:15), then applied this same request to every believer that will ever live (John 17:20)!

In Ephesians 6, Paul talks about the "armor of God" which is probably the most famous passage about protection from Satan.

He says:

> Finally, my brethren, be strong in the Lord and in the power of His might. Put on the whole armor of God, that you may be able to stand against the wiles of the devil. For we do not wrestle against flesh and blood, but against principalities, against powers, against the rulers of the darkness of this age, against spiritual hosts of wickedness in the heavenly places. Therefore take up the whole armor of God, that you may be able to withstand in the evil day, and having done all, to stand.
> *Ephesians 6:10-13*

Paul does not say we advance against, bind, or conquer any of the rulers of the darkness; we are only to stand our ground. Jesus said, "I will build my church, and the gates of Hades shall not prevail against it" (Matthew 16:18). Our job is to stand firm using the armor God gave us.

Each piece of armor is a part of our identity as believers. We have the truth, symbolized by a belt and righteousness from Christ which is symbolized by a breastplate (Ephesians 6:14). Our footwear is a way to symbolize preparedness to preach the Gospel wherever Jesus sends us (Ephesians 6:15) and we have salvation through Jesus' death which Paul says is our helmet (Ephesians 6:17). The last two pieces of equipment are a little different from the previous ones.

Paul says, "Above all, taking the shield of faith with which you will be able to quench all the fiery darts of the wicked one" (Ephesians 6:16). The most important thing we have is our faith in God and it protects us from Satan's attacks. No matter how he assaults us, our faith is what will protect us from being swayed by his deception. Our faith is not alone though; we need truth, righteousness, preparation, and salvation to accompany it in order to be effective. If we do not have each piece of armor like a battle-ready soldier, we will be vulnerable to certain attacks. If a believe—who by definition has faith—is not grounded in God's truth, his faith will be less effective to quench Satan's darts.

The last thing Paul mentions is our only offensive weapon: "the sword of the Spirit, which is the word of God" (Ephesians 6:17). The only way we can fight back against Satan is to use the Bible. In combat, if the victim only blocks an opponent's attacks, he will be beaten because the attacker will eventually will find a way through their armor or wear out his defenses. God does not want us to stand still and allow Satan to continually beat on us. He gave us a weapon to fight back so that we could become more sanctified in Him and preach the Gospel to others. All of our pieces of armor allow us to win the battles God has us fighting against Satan. Only Jesus will win the war against the devil when He returns, but we can win individual battles by standing on Scripture.

Paul concludes his passage about our armor by telling his audience to pray always "with all prayer and supplication in the Sprit, being watchful to this end with all perseverance and supplication for all the saints" (Ephesians 6:18). The armor of God is not complete if it is not coupled with prayer, both for ourselves and for all believers. Putting on the armor of God and praying will naturally make us submit to Him. Submitting to God is by definition resisting the devil and James says "he will flee from you" (James 4:7). When we do all these things, the Lord will be faithful and "will establish you and guard you from the evil one" (II Thessalonians 3:3).

Unfortunately, we don't always properly equip ourselves for battle with Satan. We make mistakes, we fall prey to his deception, and we sin. But even when that happens, God remains faithful because "He cannot deny Himself" (II Timothy 2:13). We overcome the wicked one through our faith as John wrote to his audience (I John 2:13-14). John says the victory that has overcome the world, Satan included, is our faith (I John 5:4). Even when we fail, we can be assured God has promised our victory over Satan by our faith in Him.

DEMONS

Chapter 14

The Demons' Beginning

We know from studying Satan that he has angels following and fighting with him (Revelation 12:7-9). The Bible refers to these angelic followers of Satan as demons, unclean spirits, and a few other names. God did not create Satan as evil so He must not have created demons as evil either. Where did the demons come from? The Bible does not give us a direct answer, but logically it must have happened sometime after Satan rebelled against God. Certain spirits decided to follow Satan instead of their Creator, thus becoming evil spirits which we call demons. Apparently it was one third of all the angels because Revelation 12:4 says of Satan, "His tail drew a third of the stars of heaven and threw them to the earth." The demons' home, just like Satan, is now on earth instead of heaven.

Are all demons fallen angels? We know Satan was a cherubim (Ezekiel 28:14), and does that mean some demons could be different heavenly creatures other than angels? Revelation 12:7 calls Satan's followers angels, but we are never told if his army is exclusively angels. Paul says in Ephesians 6:12 that we wrestle against principalities and powers, but this could be referring to the hierarchy of the demons rather than different creatures which we classify as demons. Suffice to say all demons are bad whether they are different creatures or not.

Chapter 15

The Demons' End

Just like the demons' beginning, the Bible doesn't give a lot of information about what happens to demons at the end of time. We know they will end up in the lake of fire because Jesus tells us the everlasting fire is prepared for the devil and his angels (Matthew 25:41). Demons also know they will eventually be sent to hell, referring to it as "the time" (Matthew 8:29). Because of these things, just like Satan, there is no salvation plan for demons.

At the end of the Tribulation, Satan is bound for a thousand years, released, and then thrown into the lake of fire (Revelation 20:2-3, 7, 10). Demons are not mentioned throughout this sequence. Does that mean demons are still on earth during the Millennium or are they bound along with Satan for one thousand years? Ultimately we don't know. I tend to think they will still be on earth during the Millennium, but I would never break fellowship over this issue. Either way, we know they will eventually be thrown in the lake of fire where they will be judged for their decision to rebel against God forever and ever.

Chapter 16

Demons Before the Flood

The first time demons are mentioned in the Old Testament is in Genesis 6:2 where they are given the title "sons of God." The phrase "sons of God" must refer to angels because the only other times the phrase is used is in Job "when the sons of God came to present themselves before the LORD, and Satan also came among them" (Job 1:6, 2:1) and Job 38:7 where, "The morning stars sang together, and all the sons of God shouted for joy." Since these are the only other passages mentioning this phrase and it refers to angels, we are left to conclude Genesis 6:2 and 6:4 must also be referring to angels. Furthermore, Genesis 6:1 mentions men and daughters and 6:2 mentions daughters of men. If Moses, the author of Genesis, wanted us to think the sons of God were ordinary men, he would have used the phrase "sons of men" to match the phrase "daughters of men."

There are many other reasons to conclude the sons of God are angels, and much has been written about the topic. But the debate isn't really over the phrase itself; it has to do with what the sons of God are doing. If the sons of God weren't doing what is hard for us to imagine, there probably wouldn't be a debate about the identity of the sons of God.

"The sons of God saw the daughters of men, that they were beautiful; and they took wives for themselves of all whom they chose... the sons of God came in to the daughters of men and they bore children to them" (Genesis 6:2, 4). Jesus said men and women in the resurrection, "neither marry nor are given in marriage, but are like the angels of God in heaven" (Matthew 22:30). If angels do not marry, that means they do not have children because sex and thus procreation outside of marriage is a sin (Exodus 20:14, Hebrews 13:4). What the sons of God did in Genesis 6 was leave their own abode (Jude 6), marry, and have children. Notice also the sons of God "took wives for themselves of all whom they chose," (Genesis 6:2), which may indicate they married more than one woman.

What is even stranger is that angels and demons, even though they do not marry, are apparently capable of reproduction with humans. This is the real debate over whether sons of God are angels: the fact of the offspring from the union of them and the daughters of men. Scientifically, the Bible gives no information how a spiritual being could fertilize a woman's egg, but apparently it is possible. A modern way to describe the children would be demon-human hybrids, which sounds much more like a pagan or occultic idea than a Biblical one. However, if we consider the motive for Satan and his demons to have children with women (not necessarily saying Satan was one of the angels who married women and had offspring), it makes sense for them to try something like this.

Satan knew his defeat would come from the Seed of the woman (Genesis 3:15). This passage not only predicts the virgin birth of Jesus, but also demands a human woman give birth to a son. Therefore, if Satan can corrupt the gene pool and make women non-human, this prophecy could not come true.

Humans should have known not to get married and have children with non-humans because God said a man and his wife shall become one flesh (Genesis 2:24), not a spirit and his wife. Both the demons and women were committing sin through this union.

For the women involved this was probably a very tempting sin; the demon-human hybrids born to women were giants and "mighty men who were of old, men of renown" (Genesis 6:4). Having an extremely powerful child would be a great way to further a family's control and authority over other people. God says the earth was corrupt and filled with violence at that time (Genesis 6:11) probably in part because these hybrid men were fighting for control over the earth. If Satan's goal is to take over and rule the earth, most likely that is what he was using his demons and their offspring to do.

When did all this start taking place? Genesis 6:1 says, "Now it came to pass, when men began to multiply on the face of the earth, and daughters were born to them." Adam and Eve had sons and daughters (Genesis 5:4) so demons could have started their marriages as soon as women were old enough to have children. "There were giants on the earth in those days" (Genesis 6:4). What days? The days when men began to multiply on the face of the earth and daughters were born to them which began with Adam and Eve's children. This is relatively clear, but the next three words in Genesis 6:4 have caused much debate: "and also afterward."

I take "and also afterward" to mean "and also afterward when men began to multiply of the face of the earth, and daughters were born to them," which means these unions were not a one time event. They kept happening all the way up until the flood. Demons kept marrying women and having children and theoretically the hybrids did the same. By the time God commanded Noah to build the ark, "the earth is filled with violence through them" (Genesis 6:13). Who is them? "All flesh had corrupted their way on the earth" (Genesis 6:12) and "every intent of the thoughts of his heart was only evil continually" (Genesis 6:5). Not only did all flesh fill the earth with violence and wickedness, but some weren't one hundred percent human.

"Noah was a just man, perfect in his generations" (Genesis 6:9). According to this verse, Noah was a believer, but also his genes were purely human and not corrupted by demon "DNA." The men in the genealogy of Genesis 5 along with their wives must have never been descendants of any demon-woman union. Does this mean every single human not part of this genealogy was a hybrid? Maybe, but the Bible doesn't give us enough information one way or the other. We can be sure there were no other believers on the planet other than Noah and his family or else they would have been on the ark. As an application to our modern day, if there were only eight believers in those days and God worked through them to bring about a population as large as it is today, it may be that we see very few believers before the Rapture or at the end of the Tribulation.

But can the phrase "and also afterward" mean "also after the flood?" This is a difficult question because the Bible does mention people after the flood that seem to be similar to the giants in Genesis 6. The most well known example is Goliath who is mentioned as both a champion and a giant (I Samuel 17:4, I Chronicles 20:4). He is also the only person in the Bible whose height is recorded; he was roughly nine feet tall or maybe a bit more (there are different standards for a cubit and span so exact height is uncertain). Goliath's sons are also mentioned although their height is not recorded. One of them is mentioned to have a large spear (I Chronicles 20:5) and another is mentioned to have great stature as well as six fingers and toes on each hand and foot respectively (I Chronicles 20:6). Does this indicate demons were having the same interactions with women as they were before the flood?

Although it is possible (if they were capable of it back then they are capable of it at any point in history), it seems unlikely. Corrupting the gene pool was a very effective strategy for Satan and his demons because they were able to corrupt all flesh through genetics and sin except for Noah and his generations within roughly 1400 years of creation. Noah, his sons, and their daughters must have been purely human, therefore the flood killed all corrupted flesh.

There is a theory that since the hybrids aren't totally human, they could have survived the flood because they are part spiritual. But being part spiritual, they are also part human, which means they would have death passed onto them (Romans 5:12) even though their seed is not from a man. They would also have a body in which their soul is connected. These qualities of being human suggest they would have physically died in the flood. However, these arguments are emphasizing the human nature of hybrids. If you emphasize their spiritual or angel part, you could have a different conclusion, but it seems the human part of their genetic makeup is dominant because they are called men in Genesis 6:4. Furthermore, God used a flood to destroy all flesh. If they were able to survive, a deluge was not an effective way for God to remove the wickedness from the earth.

We don't see a proliferation of giants and hybrids today, so its safe to conclude the demons are not still having these relations at least on a large scale. Why not? I think the best explanation is God has deterred demon-human relations. In I Peter, the author is describing Christ's suffering and how He was "put to death in the flesh but made alive by the Spirit" (I Peter 3:18). Peter then says Jesus by the Spirit, "went and preached to the spirits in prison, who formerly were disobedient, when once the Divine longsuffering waited in the days of Noah, while the ark was being prepared, in which a few, that is, eight souls, were saved through water" (I Peter 3:19-20). Who were the "spirits in prison" Jesus preached to? These are not deceased humans because people, even when in heaven or hell, or never referred to as spirits in the Bible. However, angels are often referred to as spirits. Therefore, it is probable Jesus went and preached to angels who were in prison. The spirits must be demons because the good angels would have no reason to be in prison.

But why were these demons in prison? "For if God did not spare the angels who sinned, but cast them down to hell and delivered them into chains of darkness, to be reserved for judgment" (II Peter 2:4). These spirits in prison must be the sons of God in Genesis 6 who were marrying women and having hybrid children because in the next verse Peter talks about Noah and "the flood on the world of the ungodly" (II Peter 2:5). If this is the case, God put the demons who sinned in prison because of their sin.

I would guess demons would rather be on earth working against humanity than in prison; therefore it is likely demons stopped having intercourse with women at least as a common occurence. God could have also thrown the offending demons in prison and then prohibited the remaining demons from committing the sin in the same way He did not allow Satan to kill Job (Job 2:6). These demons in prison could also be the locusts from the bottomless pit released by the fifth trumpet during the Tribulation (Revelation 9:1-3) although we can't be absolutely sure about this connection.

If God did not specifically prohibit demons from marrying women but rather used prison as only a deterrent, this could explain giants, such as Goliath, after the flood. Demons could still try committing this sin once again and maybe God sends them to prison with the others when they do. Or maybe God allows these unions on certain occasions for some reason. Could we also see a return of demons having children with women during or leading up to the Tribulation? I think that's also a possibility.

Although Genesis 6 is an important event, we should not let this small passage of Scripture with sparse details largely influence how we interpret the rest of the Bible. This means to not read the entire Bible through the lens of Genesis 6 and relate everything back to this one event. There are lots of predictions how often demon-women unions happen in history or about how it will happen in the future, such as using Jesus' mention of the days of Noah in Matthew 24:37 (Jesus' reference to this time is referring to how "normal life" was happening in Noah's days and then everyone except Noah's family was killed by a flood. In the same way, "normal life," as much as is possible during the Tribulation, will be happening, then Jesus will return and unbelievers will be killed.).

Could demons again start having children with women during the last days because of the proliferation of evil? It's a possibility, but I don't believe it is one of the main things to be concerned with when talking about prophecy because the Bible doesn't specifically mention it happening. There are many other deceptions the Bible warns about during and leading up the the Tribulation on which we should be focused, such as the signs demons will be performing. Let's continue to look at the other things demons were doing in the Old Testament.

Chapter 17

Demons in the Old Testament

Paul tells us something very important about demons in the Old Testament in the first letter to the Corinthians. He explains, "We know that an idol is nothing in the world, and that there is no other God but one. For even if there are so-called gods, whether in heaven or on earth (as there are many gods and many lords)" (I Corinthians 8:4-5). The so-called "gods" are not gods like the one true God. Are these "gods" imaginary or are they real entities? Later in Paul speaks about idols again and says, "The things which the Gentiles sacrifice they sacrifice to demons and not to God, and I do not want you to have fellowship with demons. You cannot drink the cup of the Lord and the cup of demons; you cannot partake of the Lord's table and of the table of demons" (I Corinthians 10:20-21).

Putting these verses together, idols that represent so-called "gods" are actually demons. We should not participate in idolatry (I Corinthians 10:14) because it makes us partakers with demons. Therefore, when we see gods talked about in the Old Testament or any other ancient text, those "gods" are really demons. Does that mean demons showed themselves to humans and then people started to worship them? It is certainly possible.

However, Old Testament passages also mention idols being creations of people, such as Isaiah 2:8 which says, "Their land is also full of idols; they worship the work of their own hands, that which their own fingers have made." People could also have imagined other gods just like we imagine creatures and mythical stories today, then proceeded to create images from their own thoughts. Demons could also assume the identity of these idols, a deceptive way to bring "life" to a person's imagination.

In Judges chapter 9, Abimelech the son of Gideon persuades the men of Shechem to make him king. Then he killed his seventy brothers except Jotham and became king. God allowed Abimelech to be king three years but then "sent a spirit of ill will between Abimelech and the men of Shechem; and the men of Shechem dealt treacherously with Abimelech" (Judges 9:23). While the "spirit of ill will" could have been just a feeling or mood, I take this to be an actually spirit; God used a demon to influence men to act a certain way. Why did He do this? "That the crime done to the seventy sons of Jerubbaal might be settled and their blood be laid on Abimelech their brother, who killed them, and on the men of Shechem, who aided him in the killing of his brothers" (Judges 9:24).

For the rest of Judges 9, Abimelech and the men of Shechem fight against each other. After many died and everyone who was left went home, Judges 9:56-57 says, "Thus God repaid the wickedness of Abimelech, which he had done to his father by killing his seventy brothers. And all the evil of the men of Shechem God returned on their own heads, and on them came the curse of Jotham the son of Jerubbaal." The demon God sent influenced Abimelech and the men of Shechem to eventually kill each other which was God's justice on them. Just as God uses Satan to accomplish His will, He uses demons as well.

God used another spirit in Saul's life after Goliath was defeated by David: "And it happened on the next day that the distressing spirit from God came upon Saul, and he prophesied inside the house" (I Samuel 18:10). We can assume this distressing spirit influenced Saul to try to pin David against the wall, be afraid of David, and remove him from his presence (I Samuel 18:11-16). The distressing spirit is mentioned a second time in I Samuel 19:9-10 where Saul tries to pin David to the wall again. Saul acts very erratically for the rest of his life and tries to kill David many times. The Bible doesn't say this directly, but the distressing spirit could have had a part to play in Saul's behavior for the rest of his life.

Why did God use a demon to influence Saul? We aren't told, but we do know God used Saul's behavior to sanctify David and eventually bring him up as king. During this period David also wrote many Psalms about his experiences, such as Psalm 59. If Saul did not have the influence of the demon, he might not have been chasing David for a long the time. If David had not been running from Saul, he would not have had training for his faith and God could not have used him to write parts of Scripture. God used this distressing spirit in a mighty way to bring about His will.

I Samuel 18:10 also says Saul prophesied when the spirit came upon him. What did he prophesy? We aren't told, but I think we can make a good guess. However, let's discuss the next time demons are mentioned to inform us about what Saul may have prophesied.

In II Chronicles 18:1-27, King Ahab persuades King Jehoshaphat into going to war with him against Ramoth Gilead, but Jehoshaphat wanted to inquire of God before they go. Ahab gathers four hundred prophets who all prophesy encouragement for Ahab to go and win the battle. Jehoshaphat apparently realizes that something is not right because he asks Ahab, "'Is there not still a prophet of the LORD here, that we may inquire of Him?' So the king of Israel said to Jehoshaphat, 'There is still one man by whom we may inquire of the LORD; but I hate him, because he never prophesies good concerning me, but always evil. He is Micaiah the son of Imla.'" (II Chronicles 18:6-7). Jehoshaphat is appalled at Ahab's response, and Micaiah is summoned. Before he arrives, Ahab's other prophets prophesy in the name of the LORD Ahab's victory in the battle.

The messenger of Ahab who called Micaiah tells him to agree with what the prophets have already spoken, which indicates to us what was really going on in Ahab's court: Ahab had many prophets, but they were not seeking God's Word but had other motives, chief of which was to speak well of the king. Micaiah says to the messenger, "As the LORD lives, whatever my God says, that I will speak" (I Chronicles 18:13). When Ahab asks Micaiah what to do, he replies in accordance with the other prophets: "'Go and prosper, and they shall be delivered into your hand!' So the king said to him, 'How many times shall I make you swear that you tell me nothing but the truth in the name of the LORD?'" (I Chronicles 18:14-15). In some way, the manner in which Micaiah communicated with Ahab indicated he was only repeating what he had been told by the messenger to say.

Micaiah then tells Ahab what will happen: "I saw all Israel scattered on the mountains, as sheep that have no shepherd. And the LORD said, 'These have no master. Let each return to his house in peace'" (I Chronicles 18:16). God through Micaiah warned Ahab he would be defeated in battle. Ahab then complains to Jehoshaphat that Micaiah always speaks evil concerning him, but then Micaiah tells of a vision which gives us more insight into how demons interact with God and man:

> I saw the LORD sitting on His throne, and all the host
> of heaven standing on His right hand and His left. And

Demons in the Old Testament

the LORD said, "Who will persuade Ahab king of Israel to go up, that he may fall at Ramoth Gilead?" So one spoke in this manner, and another spoke in that manner. Then a spirit came forward and stood before the LORD, and said, "I will persuade him." The LORD said to him, "In what way?" So he said, "I will go out and be a lying spirit in the mouth of all his prophets." And the LORD said, "You shall persuade him and also prevail; go out and do so."
II Chronicles 18:18-21

God had what we might call an "open panel" for demons and possibly good angels to propose their methods of how they would influence Ahab. The spirit who was chosen must have been a demon because a righteous angel would not be a lying spirit. God used this spirit—much like He used the spirits in Judges and I Samuel—to accomplish His purpose, which was to have Ahab die in battle (II Chronicles 18:27).

As a side note, the spirit in heaven is said to stand before God. While we are never given a clear description of a demon's body, we know from this passage they can stand. The demon is also referred to as a "he," indicating a male gender which would corroborate Genesis 6 in which the demons are acting as men not women.

Micaiah next gives Ahab a summary of what happened with the four hundred prophets: "Therefore look! The LORD has put a lying spirit in the mouth of these prophets of yours, and the LORD has declared disaster against you" (II Chronicles 18:22). At this point, Ahab could choose who he would believe: the prophet from God or the other prophets. God's prophets had been right many times in Ahab's life, so he had every reason to believe Micaiah. Instead, he threw him in prison. God gave Ahab a chance to change his mind even though He had allowed a demon to have influence. Ahab still had the option between faith and pride even though God foreknew his choice.

Back in I Samuel 18:10, I believe it is possible Saul prophesied what would eventually happen to him. In the same way as Ahab, God was giving Saul the option between trusting in Him for how he should treat David or pride to treat David very poorly. Even if this wasn't what Saul prophesied, God gave him many chances to turn from his behavior toward David. These situations, Ahab and Saul, are similar to Job and Peter: when God allowed demons or Satan to have an influence in their lives, He always gave them the option of faith as well. Job and Peter choose the path of faith and their lives were better for it. Ahab and Saul choose the path of pride and their lives were ended. Which will we choose?

The last time demons are mentioned in the Old Testament is in the book of Daniel. In chapter 10, Daniel is mourning because of the visions he received and his lack of understanding of them. After seeing a man with a fantastic appearance, an angel touches Daniel and begins telling him about his perilous journey to give Daniel understanding: "The prince of the kingdom of Persia withstood me twenty-one days; and behold, Michael, one of the chief princes, came to help me, for I had been left alone there with the kings of Persia" (Daniel 10:13). The princes and kings of Persia would not be able to detain an angel for three weeks, so this verse must be talking about something else. Much like the Isaiah and Ezekiel passages about Satan that are addressed to earthly kings, this passage must also be talking about spiritual beings "behind the throne" so to speak. Demons who were at least involved in Persia's affairs were able to isolate this angel and keep him from reaching Daniel until Michael came and helped.

This verse teaches us that demons are involved in earthly kingdoms. Paul could have been thinking about this same idea when he said, "For we do not wrestle against flesh and blood, but against principalities, against powers, against the rulers of the darkness of this age, against spiritual hosts of wickedness in the heavenly places" (Ephesians 6:12). Both Daniel and Ephesians indicate believers' struggles in this world are not with the people they directly deal with, but the spiritual beings who are influencing those people. From the Daniel passage, we know demons and angels are also battling against one another for either Satan's will or God's will.

The demons who are involved with kingdoms must also be able to influence government officials to use the power of the government against believers. If this is the case, demons may have influenced the governors and satraps to develop a law that would bring a charge against Daniel (Daniel 6:4-5). As we navigate our modern day, we should be very aware of spiritual influences in our own government.

We also learn demons and angels have to travel through space and interact with our time stream. Satan mentions himself as "walking back and forth" on the earth, which implies movement. Neither Satan nor demons are omnipresent, but are only in one place at one time. Theoretically, since they do not have physical bodies, they can move much faster than humans or animals, although we do not know the speeds of which they are capable or if they can simply appear somewhere else as Jesus did after the resurrection (Luke 24:36).

After a bit of conversation between Daniel and the angel, the angel told Daniel, "And now I must return to fight with the prince of Persia; and when I have gone forth, indeed the prince of Greece will come" (Daniel 10:20). Apparently this fight in which Michael helped (Daniel 10:13, 21) ended with the fall of Persia and the rise of the kingdom of Greece which began with Alexander the Great. This indicates kingdoms of the world rise and fall at least in part because of battles between angels and demons. Is this the case for every kingdom? Spiritual forces are surely a factor given what Daniel, other prophets, and Paul mention about the principalities and powers, but we must be careful before building a detailed doctrine when there are so few verses giving us information on the interaction of demons and angels with governments. Demons are clearly involved in human affairs, but are not the sole source of action. Lest we think only demons are to blame for a government's actions, the Antichrist and the False Prophet are the first ones sent to the lake a fire (Revelation 19:20), which shows judgment upon their lack of faith in God and their deeds. Humans and demons are both responsible for how kingdoms are run and we should take note of this as we see events in our world today.

Chapter 18

Demons in the Gospels

Before we get to passages in the Gospels talking specifically about demons, there are a few indirect references about demons that teach us about what people were aware of in Israel during Jesus' ministry. After feeding the five thousand, "Jesus made His disciples get into the boat and go before Him to the other side... And when the disciples saw Him walking on the sea, they were troubled, saying, 'It is a ghost!' And they cried out for fear" (Matthew 14:22, 26). The first thought the disciples have when seeing a person walking on water is to assume it was a ghost or spirit. Why did they think that? The disciples knew people can't walk on water, so this must be something else; something otherworldly is the only explanation of the shape for a man walking on water. For the disciples to think this, there must have been some common understanding in Jewish culture of what we would today call the paranormal. Even though demons are not mentioned as appearing visually in the Old Testament except for Genesis 6, they must have appeared often enough for there to be a cultural understanding of what a spirit was. Notice also the disciples were afraid of the supposed spirit. People still have the same reaction to the paranormal today because something we encounter as "other" elicits fear of what might happen to us.

After Jesus' resurrection, He stood in the midst of the disciples "and said to them, 'Peace to you.' But they were terrified and frightened and supposed they had seen a spirit" (Luke 24:36-37). Jesus' response is very interesting: "Why are you troubled? And why do doubts arise in your hearts? Behold My hands and My feet, that it is I Myself. Handle Me and see, for a spirit does not have flesh and bones as you see I have" (Luke 24:38-39). Jesus doesn't tell them they are crazy for believing spirits exist, but rather defines what a spirit isn't.

Not only do spirits exist, but they appear in forms that do not have flesh and bones. This tells us angels and demons do not have physical bodies as humans do, although they must have some sort of body because they are not omnipresent and must travel from place to place (Daniel 10:13). Humans can see angels on certain occasions (John 20:12), yet the Bible never describes humans seeing demons. Does this mean demons cannot appear in a visible way or can they appear to humans as angels do? The Bible does not give a clear answer. However, the sons of God in Genesis 6 theoretically had to appear to their wives in some visible way. If the locusts in Revelation 9:1-12 are demons, and I believe they are, John gives a description of what they look like in that form. Since demons are fallen angels, they could retain the same ability as good angels to appear as normal men or an angelic form (Genesis 18:2, Luke 2:9). Ultimately, we do not know but can reasonably infer the above possibilities.

Matthew 12:43-35 and Luke 11:24-26 discuss demon possession which we will study in a later chapter, but both authors give us this detail: the unclean spirit "goes and takes with him seven other spirits more wicked than himself." Not only are there many demons but varying degrees of wickedness among them. Even though the Bible doesn't say this, we could also infer there are demons with varying amounts of power, just as Michael seems to be more powerful than other angels because of his position as a chief prince (Daniel 10:13, Revelation 12:7). Perhaps the more wicked demons are also more powerful, which is why we see people possessed by demons having different reactions and symptoms.

Demons are able to speak in an audible way such as the demons in Mark 3:11 who "cried out, saying, 'You are the Son of God'" to Jesus. Another instance of demons talking may be the man in Mark 1:23-24 who had an unclean spirit and spoke in the presence of the synagogue, although the text does not make clear who spoke, the man or the unclean spirit inside him. Whoever did talk only spoke after Jesus' teaching rather than when Jesus entered the synagogue. It seems there is a point at which demons cannot but cry out against the Word of God, but it is not simply at the presence of believers, the Bible, or even Jesus Himself. Not only can demons speak audibly, but demon possessed people can be anywhere, even in our churches, and we may not know until until the Word of God is preached with authority.

There is no mention of demons speaking without being inside a person, so it may be that demons cannot speak audibly unless they use the vocal chords of the person they are possessing. But just like their ability to appear in a visible way, they may retain the same capacity to speak as the holy angels. What does a demon sound like when he speaks? There is no description of a demon's voice, so we cannot authoritatively say demons use the same voice as the person they are possessing or have a voice of their own. Angels seem to have normal human-like voices or can speak very loudly in a way that sounds as if

Deceiving by Signs

their voice is coming from many different places like many waters or loud thunder (Revelation 14:2). Since demons are the same creatures as angels except they rebelled against God, their voices may work the same way.

Chapter 19

Demons in the Church Age

Demons are aware of the activity of believers because the demon in Acts 19:15 says to the men who were trying to exorcism him, "Jesus I know, and Paul I know; but who are you?" We don't know if this evil spirit encountered Paul before, demons communicate with each other about believers' activity since they can find each other and work toward the same goal (Luke 11:26).

Multiple references to demons in the Epistles refer to them as ruling or having power over something. They are referenced as principalities, powers, rulers, spiritual hosts, and dignitaries (Romans 8:38, Ephesians 6:12, II Peter 2:10, Jude 8). They are not omnipotent because they cannot separate us from the love of God (Romans 8:39), nor are they more powerful than the armor God has given us (Ephesians 6:13). We are to treat them with a healthy respect however, because "angels, who are greater in power and might" than us, "do not bring a reviling accusation against them before the Lord" (II Peter 2:11). God will take care of stopping demons and we are to choose the path of faith when dealing with them.

In II Corinthians 12:7, Paul tells us he was given "a thorn in the flesh" which he says was a "messenger of Satan." We don't know exactly what this was, but it was something that physically effected Paul. If it was a messenger of Satan, this thorn could very well have been a demon that was given certain authority over Paul's body much like Satan was given authority over Job's body. If this is the case, this tells us God is still allowing demons to influence believer's physical health.

Not only is it possible they can effect us physically, but they can also influence us mentally. John says, "Do not believe every spirit, but test the spirits, whether they are of God; because many false prophets have gone out into the world" (I John 4:1). Demons, much like they did with Ahab, are whispering in people's ears, giving them information to turn them away for God. We will elaborate more on ways they are doing this in the church age in another chapter.

Chapter 20

Demons in the Eschaton

Much like Satan, demons become more influential during the Tribulation. In Revelation 9:1-12, we see some very strange creatures described as locusts. These locusts are released from the bottomless pit and begin to torment but not kill unbelievers for five months. They are described as the shape of a horse, crowns on their heads, faces like men, hair like women, lion's teeth, armor of iron, loud wings, and tails like scorpions. They torment people by stinging with their tail. They also have a king over them named Abaddon/Apollyon.

Given this description, this doesn't sound like anything manmade. Furthermore, the locusts are the result of the fifth trumpet, of which all trumpets are God ordained. The best explanation is these creatures are spiritual, maybe demons or another kind of principality. This will be a very bad five months for unbelievers; the sting of the locusts will be so painful they will wish to die but won't be allowed to (Revelation 9:4-6).

During this same time the two witnesses will be conducting their ministry (Revelation 11:3-6). The beast who ascends out of the bottomless pit, who is probably the same king over the locusts, will make war against them, eventually overcoming and killing them after they finish their testimony (Revelation 11:7). This suggests that even though the locusts will be tormenting mankind, they will also be fighting the two witness who are plaguing and devouring their enemies (Revelation 11:5-6). People will be stuck between the locusts harming them but also fighting against their common enemy. In this way the demons could deceive men into accepting massive pain in exchange for help, which really isn't help in the end. This will be a terrible time for those on earth, because the locusts and the two witnesses are two of the three woes mentioned during the Tribulation (Revelation 9:12, 11:14).

The angels and their armies who were released from the Euphrates at the sixth trumpet could also be demons (Revelation 9:13-19). Although just because these angels are killing people and unbound does not make them demons. John uses the words "demon" and "angel" throughout Revelation and in this passage demon is used in 9:20 to tell use who the people are worshiping. This passage is not clear about whether these are holy or evil angels.

The last passage to discuss is Revelation 18:2 where Babylon is said to have "become a dwelling place for demons, a prison for every foul spirit." Demons apparently gather where evil is prolific, and no spot on earth in all of history will be as evil as Babylon during the Tribulation. Just as demons are behind kingdoms of the world, they must also prefer certain places to dwell.

DEMONIC POWER

So far, we have looked at the identity of Satan and demons mostly chronologically through the Bible as well as how Satan's power becomes more prevalent as we move closer to the Tribulation. By entering into the section on demons' power, chronological organization becomes more difficult. Different powers are mentioned many times throughout the Bible; this section would be very haphazard if we looked at each verse on demons' power chronologically. Therefore, as each power appears, we will follow it's occurrences throughout the Bible. After studying each passage where the power occurs, we'll move onto the next power. There are also many crossovers between powers, such as king Saul participating in necromancy in order to know the future (divination). For passages with multiple powers, I will put them in the section that seems most representative of what is going on but also mention the other powers.

Demons are not specifically said to perform signs until Revelation 16:14. However, there are certainly inferences to demonic power, for example demons being able to communicate through objects and visions during a divination ritual or whenever pagan nations "consult their gods," provided there was communication from the demon posing as a god. Demons often use their power through humans, such as possessing them which makes the human become very strong. Given this, the Bible does not often say a demon's power is being used, but we can be reasonable sure signs beyond human ability are being performed by demons. Although it is not stated, we can also assume Satan can perform any power demons can manifest because he is more powerful than they.

We established in the previous section about demons' character that gods of other religions are demons masquerading as gods or just imagined. For those gods that are demons, God gave strict instructions not to follow them.

> When the LORD your God cuts off from before you the nations which you go to dispossess, and you displace them and dwell in their land, take heed to yourself that you are not ensnared to follow them, after they are destroyed from before you, and that you do not inquire after their gods, saying, "How did these nations serve their gods? I also will do likewise." You shall not worship the LORD your God in that way; for every abomination to the LORD which He hates they have done to their gods; for they burn even their sons and daughters in the fire to their gods. Whatever I command you, be careful to observe it; you shall not add to it nor take away from it.
> Deuteronomy 12: 29-32

God is telling the Israelites in this passage to not learn rituals for the purpose of contacting or worshiping false gods.

Immediately after this passage, God says,

> If there arises among you a prophet or a dreamer of dreams, and he gives you a sign or a wonder, and the sign

or the wonder comes to pass, of which he spoke to you, saying, "Let us go after other gods"—which you have not known—"and let us serve them," you shall not listen to the words of that prophet or that dreamer of dreams, for the LORD your God is testing you to know whether you love the LORD your God with all your heart and with all your soul... But that prophet or that dreamer of dreams shall be put to death, because he has spoken in order to turn you away from the LORD your God, who brought you out of the land of Egypt and redeemed you from the house of bondage, to entice you from the way in which the LORD your God commanded you to walk. So you shall put away the evil from your midst.
Deuteronomy 13:1-3, 5

These passages teach us two things about what happens when people serve other gods: rituals are performed to contact and/or serve them, and some arise with the ability to perform signs and wonders. This same pattern is outlined in occult teachings where a human can perform a ritual and then gain special power.

Another thing we learn from these passages is that the purpose of demonic signs and wonders is to get people to go after spiritual entities other than God. In fact, one reason God allows these signs or wonders to be performed is to test those who see it to know whether they love Him. We can know who is performing the sign and what the purpose is by asking this question: is this sign drawing me to God or away from God?

God gives us the antidote for not being deceived by these signs in Deuteronomy 13:4: "You shall walk after the LORD your God and fear Him, and keep His commandments and obey His voice; you shall serve Him and hold fast to Him." When we are focused on fearing God and obeying Him we will not be drawn away from Him by signs and wonders.

Deceiving by Signs

While these passages form the basis for our understanding of signs and wonders performed by demons, we need to address the dispensation in which it was given. God gave these commands to the Israelites and even gave the judgment of killing the person who performed the deceptive sign or wonder. This passage is part of the Mosaic law, and the Church is not under the law (Galatians 3:23-25). Nowhere in the New Testament does God tell the Church to kill it's members if they try to get other believers to worship other gods. The reason this passage is still very instructive to us is because we can apply the principles to our age.

There are many rituals in which a believer can participate that were created to serve false gods; sadly many churches host the performing of these rituals in their buildings! There are also many signs and wonders happening today that ultimately draw us away from God. With the advent of television, video streaming websites, and social media platforms, people have easy access to research and find instruction on how to perform rituals or see signs and wonders. If the Church is not equipped to know how to interpret these things, we will be drawn away from God. The best thing to do is exactly what Deuteronomy 13:4 tells us to do: fear God, keep His commandments, obey His voice, serve Him, and hold fast to Him.

We should never kill anyone promoting ungodly rituals or performing signs whether they are a believer or not. God gave this command to Israel, and it is not for the Church. However, there are admonitions for Christians to remove people from fellowship or have nothing to do with them because of their sinful ways (Romans 16:17, I Corinthians 5:11). Before having no fellowship with a believer, we should try our best to correct them if given the opportunity. However, if this is not possible or the person will not listen, our best course of action is to avoid them in order to keep ourselves pure (I Corinthians 5:7-8).

With each ritual, sign, or wonder connected with demonic power, there is always the possibility of humans faking or imagining things without demonic intervention. For example, not every one who tries to predict the future is getting information from a demonic source. We must not call everything that is strange demonic, but we should also not rule out the possibility of spiritual influences.

It is also worth noting that animals and non-living objects cannot communicate information to us under normal circumstances. The Bible is very clear that idols or objects fashioned from inanimate materials are useless, cannot profit, and cannot know or see anything (Isaiah 44:9). There is no record in the Bible of demons using or possessing objects, but there are mentions of accursed objects such as in Deuteronomy 7:26. The only reference to demons using animals is the New Testament story of demons entering pigs, but those pigs immediately jumped off a cliff. Even though there is not an abundance of Biblical evidence about demons using objects or animals, demons may be capable of using these things, especially as we move closer to the Tribulation. However, we will discuss this more in a later chapter.

Chapter 21

Divination, Dream Interpretation, Soothsaying, and Curses

The first account mentioned in the Bible in which humans receive help from a spiritual source other than God is the interpretations of the butler and baker's dreams in Genesis 40. These men were pagans and would not necessarily know Joseph worshiped a God from outside the Egyptian pantheon. The men said to Joseph, "We each have had a dream, and there is no interpreter of it," to which Joseph replied, "Do not interpretations belong to God? Tell them to me, please" (Genesis 40:8). These men sought an interpretation of their dream instead of assuming their dream had no meaning; in ancient Egyptian culture there had to be a common understanding of dreams being something special with a hidden meaning. The men also thought they needed an interpreter, which was someone other than themselves that knew how to interpret dreams. Joseph does not deny any of these ideas but instead focuses the source of the interpretation on God instead of himself. If the interpretation belongs to God, that means a human must go to Him to understand a dream.

Pharaoh had a dream in Genesis 41 and sought an interpreter

just like the butler and baker: "He sent and called for all the magicians of Egypt and all its wise men" (Genesis 41:8). Why did Pharaoh call magicians and wise men? Because these men claimed to have knowledge that could not be known through the natural world. They also had rituals in which they could demonstrate power seeming to go beyond a normal human's capabilities. Pharaoh went to them because he thought the interpretation of his dream had to come from a source other than human experience and knowledge; it had to come from somewhere else.

Pharaoh most likely had the same understanding as Joseph that interpretations of dreams come from God. However, he had a different understanding of Who God was. Egypt was a pagan polytheistic culture having many gods. The magicians and wise men would have sought an interpretation from their gods (they could have always made it up as well and said the gods gave them the interpretation). These gods, as we learned from I Corinthians 10:20, were actually demons. Therefore this is the first account in the Bible of men seeking interaction with demons for power or knowledge outside the natural world. However, by the time the Bible records this story, the magicians and wise men were already established as Pharaoh only called on them rather than creating their office. The practice of seeking demonic help for interpretation of dreams must have already been happening for some time in human history.

Since the interpretation of dreams belongs to God, neither demons nor humans could know what a dream means. Without His help, both parties can only be guess at the interpretation. The practice of dream interpretation continues until this day, so humans and demons' guesses must be at least somewhat accurate consistently for the practice to continue as long as it has and for someone like Pharaoh to rely on it. As with all knowledge demons give to humans about the future, their guesses can be

Divination, Dream Interpretation, Soothsaying, and Curses

pretty accurate, but the truth always remains with God.

In Pharaoh's case, the magicians and wise men were unable to produce an interpretation of his dreams (Genesis 40:8). Either the demons didn't speak for one reason or another or the magicians couldn't invent a plausible explanation. This caused Pharaoh's butler to remember Joseph and Joseph was called before Pharaoh to interpret the dream (Genesis 40:9-14). Joseph, being a righteous man, says he is not capable of understanding the dream but, "God will give Pharaoh an answer of peace" (Genesis 41:16). After hearing the dreams, he reiterates twice "God has shown Pharaoh what He is about to do" (Genesis 41:25, 28). Joseph not only attributes the interpretation to God, but he also gives God the credit for giving the dream to Pharaoh and knowing the future.

God is in control of the future and therefore the only One who knows what will happen. Any attempt by any other being to predict the future is only a guess. God did give Israel a standard for whom to believe when making predictions about the future in Deuteronomy 13:1-5 which we referenced earlier. God recognizes prophets and dreamers of dreams will be capable of making accurate predictions of the future and performing signs and wonders. Their ability is not the main thing to question although we should always be on guard against trickery. We test the purpose of the prophet or dreamer, whether they support our walk with God or try to get us to go after other gods.

Modern prophets and dreamers may not be trying to get us to follow another god directly but rather other philosophies, ideologies, or any other -ology that does not align with the Bible. Modern prophets include Nostradamus, Edgar Cayce, the Mayan calendar, or even government agencies predicting what the world will soon be like. A prophet does not have to be aligned with a religious system, but rather is anyone who predicts the future, has a vision, or gives a sign or wonder. We should always be looking for the intent of a prediction or sign and whether it brings us closer or farther away to God.

Later in Joseph's life, he uses the practice of divination as a cover to catch his brothers. The first time he sees them "he acted as a stranger to them and spoke roughly to them... Then Joseph remembered the dreams which he had dreamed about them" (Genesis 42:7, 9). It may be that Joseph treated them roughly out of anger and thought about using his power as second-in-command over Egypt to punish them. When he remembered his dreams and what they meant, it could have calmed his anger and helped him realize God's purpose was higher than his own.

Joseph accuses his brothers of being spies and treats them poorly but also weeps at hearing them talk about their sin against him. After their meeting, he gives them food, and returns their money (Genesis 42:13-25). The second time they come with Benjamin, Joseph puts his silver cup in Benjamin's sack and claims it is the cup he uses for divination (Genesis 44:5, 15).

This is the first mention in Scripture of an object being used to aid in a non-Godly spiritual ritual. I don't think Joseph actually practiced divination or that he used objects to do so. Joseph was a righteous man and would not be involved in this practice. More likely he was using this reasoning to keep his brothers unaware of his true identity. Objects are still used to practice divination today, such as tarot cards, crystal balls, or any number of other objects. Even God sometimes used objects to give His people signs or to give a prophecy, such as Agabus using Paul's belt to describe Paul's fate (Acts 21:10-11).

However, now that the written Scripture is complete (Jude 3, Revelation 22:18-19), there is no more need for any objects to be used in predicting the future or any more prophecies to be given. All we need to know, not necessarily all we want to know,

Divination, Dream Interpretation, Soothsaying, and Curses

is contained in the Bible. There is no need to go to anyone or anything other than Bible for information about the future. There is nothing wrong with making predictions on details of how certain future events the Bible already predicts will take shape; that is a useful thing to do to prepare ourselves against Satan's deception and we will be doing exactly that later in this book. But no other source need be consulted for truth. Even the Israelites were told not to practice divination or soothsaying (Leviticus 19:26).

In Numbers 22-24, Balaam and his prophecies are the next account in which divination is involved. Balak hired Balaam the soothsayer (Joshua 13:22) originally to curse the children of Israel: "Curse this people for me, for they are too mighty for me. Perhaps I shall be able to defeat them and drive them out of the land, for I know that he whom you bless is blessed, and he whom you curse is cursed" (Numbers 22:6). A curse in this sense is using spiritual forces to make bad things happen to a person or group of people. Balaam started out by listening to God and declined the proposition; yet in the end he went against what God said and accepted Balak's offer. Balaam "loved the wages of unrighteousness" (II Peter 2:15). His greed for the money Balak was paying him was too great for him to listen to God (Jude 11).

God even used Balaam's "dumb donkey speaking with a man's voice" to restrain "the madness of the prophet" (II Peter 2:16, Numbers 22:28-30). Balaam recognized his sin, and God forced him to pronounce a blessing on Israel four times instead of cursing them. Balaam even avoided using sorcery—used in this passage as another way to describe divination—after the first two prophecies, seeing that it pleased God to bless Israel (Numbers 24:1). Even through these four forced prophecies, Balaam did not heed God's Word.

We learn in Revelation about "the doctrine of Balaam, who

taught Balak to put a stumbling block before the children of Israel, to eat things sacrificed to idols, and to commit sexual immorality" (Revelation 2:14). Even after God's prophecies of blessing for Israel, Balaam's greed still drove his actions. Since divination didn't work, Balaam came up with another way to earn Balak's money. The two of them devised a plan to entice the Israelites away from God by giving them their women and inviting the people to sacrifice to their gods (Number 25:1-2). How this plan impacted the children of Israel is told in Numbers 25. God ordered everyone who committed sins with Moab and Midian to be killed. These sins were so serious that a plague was sent. Eventually Phinehas killed an Israelite man and a Midianite women while they were having sex in the sight of Moses and the congregation of the children of Israel. In the end, twenty-four thousand people died.

From the whole story of Balaam, we see greed as a chief motivator for performing divination. We also see the answers received from the practice were not desirable, so a plan was created to try to force the outcome Balak wanted and Balaam's greed satisfied. We should learn from this story that the motivations of men can impact how they seek wisdom from spiritual sources when the spiritual source is not God.

Beyond the instruction given in Deuteronomy 13:1-5 we went over at the beginning of this section, God gave additional instruction though Moses to the Israelites about divination in Deuteronomy 18:

> You shall be blameless before the LORD your God. For these nations which you will dispossess listened to soothsayers and diviners; but as for you, the LORD your God has not appointed such for you. The LORD your God will raise up for you a Prophet like me from your midst, from your brethren. Him you shall hear, according

to all you desired of the LORD your God in Horeb in the day of the assembly, saying, "Let me not hear again the voice of the LORD my God, nor let me see this great fire anymore, lest I die." And the LORD said to me: "What they have spoken is good. I will raise up for them a Prophet like you from among their brethren, and will put My words in His mouth, and He shall speak to them all that I command Him. And it shall be that whoever will not hear My words, which He speaks in My name, I will require it of him. But the prophet who presumes to speak a word in My name, which I have not commanded him to speak, or who speaks in the name of other gods, that prophet shall die." And if you say in your heart, "How shall we know the word which the LORD has not spoken?"— when a prophet speaks in the name of the LORD, if the thing does not happen or come to pass, that is the thing which the LORD has not spoken; the prophet has spoken it presumptuously; you shall not be afraid of him."
Deuteronomy 18:13-22

God did not want the Israelites participating with diviners or soothsayers because He was going to raise up a Prophet, Jesus Himself, for them to hear (Acts 3:22-23). If they listened to other prophets, they would not regard the word of God's Prophet.

God's accuracy for predictions about the future is always one hundred percent as this passage says. Therefore, if a prophet claimed to speak for God, but their prediction about the future was wrong, clearly God was not the One who told them what would happen. Even if a prophet only got one prediction wrong, the Israelites were to put that prophet to death and not be afraid of them and, by extension, their prophecies. Unfortunately, Israel did not listen to only prophets who truly spoke for God and judgment was brought upon them. While the Church is not instructed to put false prophets to death, we should follow the principle of not listening or fearing prophets whose predictions do not come true, even if those diviners are inside the Church!

Fast forward to I Samuel 6:2 where the Philistines consulted the priests and diviners about what to do with the ark of the covenant. We see here telling the future is not just about interpreting a dream or making an exact prediction of what will happen; it is also seeking advice for what to do. In the story of the Philistine priests and diviners, God ends up using their prediction as a way to confirm He was responsible for their troubles (I Samuel 6:9, 12).

God does the same thing in Ezekiel 21 when Nebuchadnezzar used divination to decide who to attack. God not only used Babylon's practice of divination to ensure they went the direction He wanted, but He even created the situation.

> And son of man, appoint for yourself two ways for the sword of the king of Babylon to go; both of them shall go from the same land. Make a sign; put it at the head of the road to the city. Appoint a road for the sword to go to Rabbah of the Ammonites, and to Judah, into fortified Jerusalem. For the king of Babylon stands at the parting of the road, at the fork of the two roads, to use divination: he shakes the arrows, he consults the images, he looks at the liver. In his right hand is the divination of Jerusalem: to set up battering rams, to call for a slaughter, to lift the voice with shouting, to set battering rams against the gates, to heap up a siege mound, and to build a wall. And it will be to them like a false divination in the eyes of those who have sworn oaths with them; but he will bring their iniquity to remembrance, that they may be taken.
> *Ezekiel 21:19-23*

Divination, Dream Interpretation, Soothsaying, and Curses

Verse 23 is not completely clear who the "thems" are, but some group of people thought the answer Nebuchadnezzar received from divination was wrong. However, God did not allow their influence to persuade the king, if they had any, to change his course of action because God had determined to punish Jerusalem for their iniquity (Ezekiel 21:24). In this passage we also see Nebuchadnezzar using various objects to get answers from his Babylonian gods or, more plainly, demons. This would have been a common practice for the Babylonians and demons very well could have manipulated the objects or shown visions through them in order to communicate knowledge.

In the previous section we talked about I Kings 22:19-23 and the lying spirit that was in the mouth of Ahab's prophets. This reference tells us very specifically that demons speak lies about the future to people. When a spirit is willing to lie, the possibilities are endless for how Satan and his demons can give humans deceptive prophecies in order to make them do what they want.

Ahaziah, the son of Ahab, did not learn from his father's missteps because we see in II Kings 1:2 he sent messengers to "inquire of Baal-Zebub, the god of Ekron" to see whether he would recover from his injury because of which he was bedridden. God was not happy about this and sent Elijah to give the messengers the real prophecy of the future. Elijah tells them, "Is it because there is no God in Israel that you are going to inquire of Baal-Zebub, the god of Ekron? Now therefore, thus says the LORD: 'You shall not come down from the bed to which you have gone up, but you shall surely die'" (II Kings 1:3-4). Ahaziah attempts to bring Elijah to himself, and after two tries of sending army captains, the third is successful (II Kings 1:9-15). Maybe Ahaziah thought he could talk Elijah into changing

God's mind, but he still died according to God's word (II Kings 1:17). Here we see God's prediction of the future is always accurate while inquiring of another god would only have been a guess. Ahaziah did not heed the proverb, "Divination is on the lips of the king; his mouth must not transgress in judgment" (Proverbs 16:10).

The prophets in the Bible who wrote down their prophecies talked a lot about diviners in Israel and what God thinks of them. Spoken through Isaiah, the practice of divination or soothsaying did not come from God: "For You have forsaken Your people, the house of Jacob, because they are filled with eastern ways; they are soothsayers like the Philistines, and they are pleased with the children of foreigners" (Isaiah 2:6). A practice God did not ordain should be enough evidence not to be involved in it. Diviners are also mentioned in Isaiah 3:2 as something taken away from Israel "because their tongue and their doings are against the LORD, to provoke the eyes of His glory" (Isaiah 3:8). Isaiah 44:25 says God is the One "Who frustrates the signs of the babblers, and drives diviners mad; Who turns wise men backward, and makes their knowledge foolishness."

God spoke to Jeremiah very strongly about diviners in Jeremiah 14:

> And the LORD said to me, "The prophets prophesy lies in My name. I have not sent them, commanded them, nor spoken to them; they prophesy to you a false vision, divination, a worthless thing, and the deceit of their heart. Therefore thus says the LORD concerning the prophets who prophesy in My name, whom I did not send, and who say, 'Sword and famine shall not be in this land'—'by sword and famine those prophets shall be consumed! And the people to whom they prophesy shall be cast out in the streets of Jerusalem because of the

famine and the sword; they will have no one to bury them —them nor their wives, their sons nor their daughters— for I will pour their wickedness on them.'"
Jeremiah 14:14-16

We know demons are willing to lie in prophecies, and now we see men are also willing to lie. Furthermore, God pronounces judgment not only on the lying prophets but also on the people who listened to them.

In Ezekiel God says of false prophets,

"They have envisioned futility and false divination, saying, 'Thus says the LORD!' But the LORD has not sent them; yet they hope that the word may be confirmed. Have you not seen a futile vision, and have you not spoken false divination? You say, 'The LORD says,' but I have not spoken." Therefore thus says the Lord GOD: "Because you have spoken nonsense and envisioned lies, therefore I am indeed against you," says the Lord GOD. "My hand will be against the prophets who envision futility and who divine lies; they shall not be in the assembly of My people, nor be written in the record of the house of Israel, nor shall they enter into the land of Israel. They you shall know that I am the Lord GOD.'"
Ezekiel 13:6-9

God clearly does not think highly of anyone using divination to speak in His name.

God also mentions the objects the prophets were using in their divination:

Woe to the women who sew magic charms on their sleeves and make veils for the heads of the people of every height to hunt souls! Will you hunt the souls of

> My people, and keep yourselves alive?... Behold, I am against your magic charms by which you hunt souls there like birds. I will tear them from your arms, and let the souls go, the souls you hunt like birds.
> Ezekiel 13:18, 20

Magic charms in Ezekiel's day would not be unlike "lucky charms" in ours; both are objects used to lead people away from trust in God and instead trust in futility and false divination. God is clearly against any object used in practices that are against Him.

God says again to the false prophets,

> Because with lies you have made the heart of the righteous sad, whom I have not made sad; and you have strengthened the hands of the wicked, so that he does not turn from his wicked ways to save his life. Therefore you shall no longer envision futility nor practice divination; for I will deliver My people out of your hand, and you shall know that I am the LORD.
> Ezekiel 13:22-23

In this passage we see another reason God hates divination: it makes the righteous sad and strengthens the wicked. The righteous know the prophecy is not from God, which saddens them because the people are not following God and lives have been made worse. The wicked are strengthened because the false prophets are justifying their wickedness in whatever form it takes. If they do not see their wickedness as wrong, they will not turn from it to be saved both from God's temporal judgment and eternal judgment.

In Ezekiel 22 there is another condemnation of Israel in which God states, "The conspiracy of her prophets in her midst is like a roaring lion tearing the prey... Her prophets plastered them with untempered mortar, seeing false visions, and divining

Divination, Dream Interpretation, Soothsaying, and Curses

lies for them, saying, 'Thus says the Lord GOD,' when the LORD had not spoken" (Ezekiel 22:25, 28). How forceful is the imagery of lions tearing at prey and a building plastered with untempered mortar for what divination did to the nation of Israel.

God also spoke through Micah about divination:

> Thus says the LORD concerning the prophets who make my people stray; who chant "Peace" while they chew with their teeth, but who prepare war against him who puts nothing into their mouths: "Therefore you shall have night without vision, and you shall have darkness without divination; the sun shall go down on the prophets, and the day shall be dark for them. So the seers shall be ashamed, and the diviners abashed; indeed they shall all cover their lips; for there is no answer from God." But truly I am full of power by the Spirit of the LORD, and of justice and might, to declare to Jacob his transgression and to Israel his sin. Now hear this, you heads of the house of Jacob and rulers of the house of Israel, who abhor justice and pervert all equity, who build up Zion with bloodshed and Jerusalem with iniquity: her heads judge for a bribe, her priests teach for pay, and her prophets divine for money. Yet they lean on the LORD, and say, "Is not the LORD among us? No harm can come upon us."
> *Micah 3:5-11*

What God makes clear in this passage is divination when done for money does not prophesy anything negative. The prophets were not receiving any message from God, and they probably wanted to keep their jobs or not die, so they would always prophesy good things to their employers, the kings of Israel. This type of divination was important enough to mention as something that would be removed when Israel was conquered by Assyria: "I will cut off sorceries from you hand, and you shall have no soothsayers" (Micah 5:12).

We see prophecies being bought again in Nehemiah 6:10-14 when Shemaiah tells Nehemiah to go into the temple to hide from Tobiah and Sanballat. Nehemiah refuses and then perceives,

> God had not sent him at all, but that he pronounced this prophecy against me because Tobiah and Sanballat had hired him. For this reason he was hired, that I should be afraid and act that way and sin, so that they might have cause for an evil report, that they might reproach me. My God, remember Tobiah and Sanballat, according to these their works, and the prophetess Noadiah and the rest of the prophets who would have made me afraid.
> *Nehemiah 6:12-14*

The Bible does not say Shemaiah's prophecy was given by using a ritual or demons communicating with them, but we can see predictions of the future not from God can be made for bribes.

Jeremiah reminds Israel to not listen to diviners after they were taken captive by Nebuchadnezzar:

> For thus says the LORD of hosts, the God of Israel: Do not let you prophets and your diviners who are in your midst deceive you, nor listen to your dreams which you cause to be dreamed. For they prophesy falsely to you in My name; I have not sent them, says the LORD.
> *Jeremiah 29:8-9*

Right before He gives the nation very uplifting words in verses 11-14, God reminds them not to listen to any prophet who does not align with the message He gave through Jeremiah.

Prophecies from God were often bad news for the kings of Israel because God judged their sin.

Divination, Dream Interpretation, Soothsaying, and Curses

> "And it shall be, that the nation and kingdom which will not serve Nebuchadnezzar the king of Babylon, and which will not put its neck under the yoke of the king of Babylon, that nation I will punish," says the LORD, "with the sword, the famine, and the pestilence, until I have consumed them by his hand. Therefore do not listen to your prophets, your diviners, your dreamers, your soothsayers, or your sorcerers, who speak to you, saying, 'You shall not serve the king of Babylon.' For they prophesy a lie to you, to remove you far from your land; and I will drive you out, and you will perish... I also spoke to Zedekiah king of Judah according to all these words, saying, 'Bring your necks under the yoke of the king of Babylon, and serve him and his people, and live!'"
> *Jeremiah 27:8-10, 12*

But even when the prophecy was for their benefit, such as blessing by serving Nebuchadnezzar, they did not listen; they did not want to do what God said. Instead they listened to the lying prophets and God drove them out (Jeremiah 27:14-15).

Zechariah tells his audience, "For the idols speak delusion; the diviners envision lies, and tell false dreams; they comfort in vain. Therefore the people wend their way like sheep; they are in trouble because there is no shepherd" (Zechariah 10:2). Lies from diviners or demons through diviners do not ultimately comfort or guide people. They make a man feel good in the moment because of a positive prophecy, but in the end the lie does not draw him nearer to God.

Daniel, much like Joseph, had to interpret the dreams and visions of rulers for whom he worked. God gave Daniel and his friends, Hananiah, Mishael, and Azariah, "knowledge and skill in all literature and wisdom; and Daniel had understanding in all visions and dreams... And in all matters of wisdom and understanding about which the king examined them, he found them ten times better than all the magicians and astrologers who were in his realm" (Daniel 1:17, 20). Why were Daniel and his friends so much better? Because they had stayed faithful to God by not participating in the same rituals and understanding as the magicians and astrologers. They surely would have been taught the practices of divination and many other things (Daniel 1:5), but they kept themselves pure.

Daniel's understanding of visions and dreams was put to the test in Daniel 2 when Nebuchadnezzar had a dream and demanded an interpretation. Unlike Pharaoh for Joseph, Nebuchadnezzar did not reveal his dream, but expected his wise men to tell him what the dream was and give an interpretation. This had not been done before as far as the history the Bible records. God reveals the secret to Daniel (Daniel 2:19), but before Daniel interprets the dream for the king, he makes sure Nebuchadnezzar knows how the whole situation came about:

> The secret which the king has demanded, the wise men, the astrologers, the magicians, and the soothsayers cannot declare to the king. But there is a God in heaven who reveals secrets, and He has made known to king Nebuchadnezzar what will be in the latter days... And He who reveals secrets has made known to you what will be. But as for me, this secret has not been revealed to me because I have more wisdom than anyone living, but for our sakes who make known the interpretation to the king, and that you may know the thoughts of your heart.
> Daniel 2:27-28, 29-30

Not only did Daniel reveal the dream, interpret it correctly, and get promoted, he also saved the lives of all the wise men under

Divination, Dream Interpretation, Soothsaying, and Curses

Nebuchadnezzar (Daniel 2:46-49). This probably created a lot of tension between Daniel and his friends and the wise men which led to spying and other devious acts (Daniel 3:8-12, 6:1-9).

Nebuchadnezzar had another vision in Daniel 4 that he told to Daniel and expected an interpretation. Daniel 4:19 says, "Daniel, whose name was Belteshazzar, was astonished for a time, and his thoughts troubled him. So the king spoke, and said, 'Belteshazzar, do not let the dream or its interpretation trouble you.' Belteshazzar answered and said, 'My lord, may the dream concern those who hate you, and its interpretation concern your enemies!'" From this passage, it seems Daniel and Nebuchadnezzar had developed a friendship because Daniel was reticent to explain the vision. However, the king was prepared for a bad interpretation. How amazing that a pagan king who was mightier than all the kings of Israel was willing to hear a negative prophecy when it was the truth rather than lies in his favor. Daniel proceeds to explain the dream and Nebuchadnezzar's future went exactly how Daniel said it would (Daniel 4:20-37).

While there may have been other times Daniel interpreted dreams or visions that weren't recorded, his final display of the understanding God gave him was for Belshazzar in Daniel 5. After the writing on the wall appeared, the wise men and astrologers were brought in but could not interpret the writing (Daniel 5:8). Daniel was brought forth, who was an old man by this time, and gave Belshazzar a history lesson on how God dealt with his father when he did not humble himself before God (Daniel 5:17-28). Daniel gave the interpretation and Babylon fell that very night (Daniel 5:30).

In these three stories, God showed His superiority to the divination practices of the wise men of the kingdom of Babylon. When God predicts the future, things will happen exactly as He says. Furthermore, God has completed His revelation of the future to mankind, so there are no new prophecies happening today. Whenever we hear a prediction or a vision of the future the Bible doesn't specifically speak on, we should always consult His Word first to verify whether it is possible or not.

The only direct mention of divination in the New Testament is in Acts when Paul encountered it:

> Now it happened, as we went to prayer, that a certain slave girl possessed with a spirit of divination met us, who brought her masters much profit by fortune-telling. This girl followed Paul and us, and cried out, saying, "These men are the servants of the Most High God, who proclaim to us the way of salvation." And this she did for many days. But Paul, greatly annoyed, turned and said to the spirit, "I command you in the name of Jesus Christ to come out of her." And he came out that very hour.
> *Acts 16:16-18*

It isn't until this passage that we learn demons specifically focused on divination can indwell people to give them the ability to tell the future. We know that the demons are only making guesses, but it is possible a spirit of divination can work with other demons to orchestrate events to bring about the future they predict, thus ensuring their "prophecies" come true. The indwelt girl was apparently good at her job because her masters made a lot of money off her prophecies. Its reasonable to assume her predictions came true often enough to keep the practice profitable. As with Balaam and many other false prophets in the Old Testament, money is often a driving force to predict a good future for those who will pay.

If demons communicated their guesses of future events when the Bible was being written, they are certainly capable of doing so now. Divination is still a common ritual today with many different names, and we have no passage indicating God's attitude toward it has changed. Believers should not be involved in any practice trying to predict the future apart from learning what God has already spoken about it.

Chapter 22

Magic, Sorcery, and Witchcraft

From the previous chapter, we see humans—especially royalty—have an interest in knowing the future, and demons are happy to oblige these requests. But humans also want power, just like Satan wants power over creation. Throughout history nations have constantly sought to gain power over another people. In order to do this, one nation's strength and/or wisdom must be greater than the other. If there is a way to gain more power, humans often seek it out. Just as demons can be involved in predicting the future, they can give people abilities not available through natural means. Power, signs, or wonders from demons through humans are called magic, sorcery, conjuring spells, or witchcraft in the Bible and these terms are still used to describe this form of power today. God displays His power in many ways throughout Scripture, such as the parting of the Red Sea or Jesus healing people's infirmities. Demons have the ability to change or manipulate the created world as well, which ultimately is what we call magic.

The most concentrated display of magic, and God's

Deceiving by Signs

superiority to it, is the magicians of Egypt and their encounters with Moses and Aaron. God made Moses as God to Pharaoh and Aaron as his prophet (Exodus 7:1) and purposed to use signs and wonders to make the Egyptians know the I AM is the true God (Exodus 7:3-5). But Pharaoh had his own gods with which he would try to combat God's power.

The first battle is during the second meeting Moses had with Pharaoh. God told Moses Pharaoh would ask for a miracle (Exodus 7:9), probably to validate whether the God to whom the Hebrews wanted to sacrifice was real and powerful.

> So Moses and Aaron went in to Pharaoh, and they did so, just as the LORD commanded. And Aaron cast down his rod before Pharaoh and before his servants, and it became a serpent. But Pharaoh also called the wise men and the sorcerers; so the magicians of Egypt, they also did in like manner with their enchantments. For every man threw down his rod, and they became serpents.
> *Exodus 7:10-12*

No one doubts God turned Aaron's rod into a serpent; He is certainly capable of this kind of power. This may be a little beyond the text, but when the miracle happened, Pharaoh does not seem impressed because he called his magicians and they were able to copy the miracle. While we could try to call this an illusion or some kind of other trick, God validates the magicians' power because "Aaron's rod swallowed up their rods" (Exodus 7:12). The magicians were able to transform their rods into serpents with their enchantments just as Aaron's rod became a serpent.

The magicians had to use enchantments to accomplish this, which means they had to use a ritual of some kind. If humans cannot turn wood into creatures, which the Bible and our human experience corroborates, then some other source of

Magic, Sorcery, and Witchcraft

power must be used to perform the miracle. The enchantments were a way to call on demons to use their power for the magicians' purpose.

Pharaoh was testing the Hebrew God and His strength against his gods' strength. Therefore he would call on his gods, who were demons, through his magicians to display their power against the Hebrew God's power. The magicians were able to turn their rods into serpents, which means demons are capable of manipulating matter in fantastic ways.

Thus began the ten plagues of Egypt, in which the first was God telling Moses,

> Say to Aaron, "Take your rod and stretch out your hand over the waters of Egypt, over their streams, over their rivers, over their ponds, and over all their pools of water, that they may become blood. And there shall be blood throughout all the land of Egypt, both in buckets of wood and pitchers of stone."
> *Exodus 7:19*

Yet after God performed the miracle, Exodus 7:22 says, "Then the magicians of Egypt did so with their enchantments." Again we see the magicians using enchantments to call upon demons' power in order to manipulate matter. In the same way Aaron performed an action—stretching his rod over the waters of Egypt—but God did the miracle—turning water into blood—the magicians performed an action and demons used their power to perform the miracle.

For the second plague, God brought forth frogs from the waters of Egypt to come over the land (Exodus 8:5). "And the magicians did so with their enchantments, and brought up frogs on the land of Egypt" (Exodus 8:7). Again the magicians were able to copy God's miracle although for this sign and the preceding one it is very likely there was a difference in magnitude or quality. My guess is that even though the magicians were able to produce frogs and blood, there was a very stark difference in the two miracles.

God created lice out of the dust of the land for the third plague (Exodus 8:16-17). "Now the magicians so worked with their enchantments to bring forth lice, but they could not" (Exodus 8:18). Why could the magicians and their demons not copy this miracle? We don't know, except we learn there is a limit to the power of demons when manipulating matter. Even the magicians admitted to Pharaoh, "This is the finger of God" (Exodus 8:19). They also perceived a limit to their enchantments, yet they recognized the Spiritual Being working through Moses and Aaron was a powerful God. This does not mean they gave up their pagan beliefs, but they recognized the Hebrew God was greater than theirs.

During the sixth plague, the plague of boils, the magicians are mentioned again: "And the magicians could not stand before Moses because of the boils, for the boils were on the magicians and on all the Egyptians" (Exodus 9:11). It could be that during the fourth and fifth plagues the magicians still tried to copy the miracles of God or were still whispering in Pharaoh's ear. But the boils were so bad they had to excuse themselves because of them.

The magicians are not mentioned again, but we know after nine of the ten plagues "the man Moses was very great in the land of Egypt, in the sight of Pharaoh's servants and in the sight of the people" (Exodus 11:3). Pharaoh's servants would have included the magicians. This could be the fulfillment of God making Moses like a God to Pharaoh and Pharaoh's servants recognized this as well. After all the plagues there may have been magicians who tried to contact the Hebrew God to get the same power Moses and Aaron possessed in the same way Simon the sorcerer tried to buy power (Acts 8:18-19). Some of the magicians might have been the servants who feared the word of the LORD and made their servants and livestock flee to their houses during the plauge of hail (Exodus 9:20). Most likely the magicians did not lose their status before Pharaoh nor did they forsake their gods, yet God showed in a mighty way His superior power to their magic.

The next time magic or sorcery is mentioned is Exodus 22:18, where the Israelites are commanded, "You shall not permit a sorceress to live." Sorcery and magic will lead people away from God, and the Israelites were not to participate in it just as they were not to participate in divination (Leviticus 19:26). While we don't kill anyone for being a sorceress today, God commanded the Israelites to remove the temptation of sorcery by killing anyone who praciced the art. King Saul carried out this command which the medium at En Dor confirms: "Then the woman said to him, 'Look, you know what Saul has done, how he has cut off the mediums and the spiritists from the land" (I Samuel 28:9). We also learn from this passage a sorceress could also be called a medium or spiritist, which is a person who contacts spirits and communicates with them. We will discuss mediums and familiar spirits in another chapter.

I Samuel 15:22-23 teaches us that in God's eyes, humans participating in witchcraft is the same as rebelling against Him:

> So Samuel said: "Has the LORD as great delight in burnt offerings and sacrifices, as in obeying the voice of the LORD? Behold, to obey is better than sacrifice, and to heed than the fat of rams. For rebellion is as the sin of witchcraft, and stubbornness is as iniquity and idolatry. Because you have rejected the word of the LORD, He also has rejected you from being king."
> *I Samuel 15:22-23*

Deceiving by Signs

Samuel spoke these words after Saul did not utterly destroy the Amalekites but took some of their spoil (I Samuel 15:18-19). Witchcraft is very closely related if not the same as sorcery which the children of Israel should have been familiar with through the stories of the Exodus; it was a very bad sin and Saul knew it which was why the comparison was so forceful.

In I Kings 16:31, we read about king Ahab: "And it came to pass, as though it had been a trivial thing for him to walk in the sins of Jeroboam the son of Nebat, that he took as wife Jezebel the daughter of Ethbaal, king of the Sidonians; and he went and served Baal and worshiped him." Jezebel was certainly a pagan, but there was also something else about her of note.

In II Kings 9, king Jehu is being used by God to strike down the house of Ahab to "avenge the blood of My servants the prophets, and the blood of all the servants of the LORD, at the hand of Jezebel" (II Kings 9:7). Later, when Joram meets Jehu and asks if he is peaceful, Jehu replies, "What peace, as long as the harlotries of your mother Jezebel and her witchcraft are so many?" (II Kings 9:22). Jezebel not only killed God's prophets, but was a witch. Her witchcraft must have strongly influenced the royalty during her life, and her deeds earned her a violent death (II Kings 9:10, 30-37). Jezebel's witchcraft was probably not the only influence, but Ahab's family was so corrupt that God destroyed all of them (II Kings 10:17).

King Manasseh was a very wicked king who participated in a host of abominations that other nations practiced: "He made his son pass through the fire, practiced soothsaying, used witchcraft, and consulted spiritists and mediums. He did much evil in the sight of the LORD, to provoke Him to anger" (II Kings 21:6). Witchcraft is mentioned alongside other demonically influenced practices to show how evil Manasseh's works were. Apparently he

Magic, Sorcery, and Witchcraft

practiced these things to such a degree that he was more wicked than the Amorites (II Kings 21:11). God allowed him to reign for fifty-five years before He brought calamity on Jerusalem and Judah because of Manasseh's wickedness (II Kings 21:1, 12).

The prophets also mentioned magic when they gave their messages to Israel. In Micah 5:12, God says, "I will cut off sorceries from your hand, and you shall have no soothsayers" when the Messiah executes judgment on the nations. God pronounces judgment on sorcerers when John the Baptist came by saying, "I will come near you for judgment; I will be a swift witness against sorcerers, against adulterers, against perjurers, against those who exploit wage earners and widows and orphans, and against those who turn away an alien— because they do not fear Me" (Malachi 3:5). We should take heed that sorcery is mentioned alongside other sins such as adultery and not paying people fairly. While witchcraft is very bad, from God's perspective there is a sense of equality; sin is sin.

God even pronounces judgment on foreign nations because of their sorceries. He says of Babylon,

> But these two things shall come to you in a moment, in one day: the loss of children, and widowhood. They shall come upon you in their fullness because of the multitude of your sorceries, for the great abundance of your enchantments... Stand now with your enchantments and the multitude of your sorceries, in which you have labored from your youth— perhaps you will be able to profit, perhaps you will prevail.
> *Isaiah 47:9, 12*

In other passages, God mentions other reasons Babylon will be destroyed, but sorcery is one of top reasons. God also pronounced judgment on Nineveh "because of the multitude of harlotries of the seductive harlot, the mistress of sorceries, who

143

sells nations through her harlotries, and families through her sorceries" (Nahum 3:4).

In the New Testament we meet Simon the sorcerer:

> There was a certain man called Simon, who previously practiced sorcery in the city and astonished the people of Samaria, claiming that he was someone great, to whom they all gave heed, from the least to the greatest, saying, "This man is the great power of God." And they heeded him because he had astonished them with his sorceries for a long time.
> *Acts 8:9-11*

There is no indication in this passage that Simon's sorcery was only illusions or slight of hand tricks; he was a real sorcerer with real power. He used his sorcery to perform signs which gained him status among the people.

> Then Simon himself also believed; and when he was baptized he continued with Philip, and was amazed, seeing the miracles and signs which were done... And when Simon saw that through the laying on of the apostles' hands the Holy Spirit was given, he offered them money, saying, "Give me this power also, that anyone on whom I lay hands may receive the Holy Spirit."
> *Acts 8:13, 18-19*

Simon, who we know already had a taste of supernatural power and wanted to be someone great, saw another power through the apostles and wanted it also. He probably saw Philip using the power of the Holy Spirit, which included the ability to exorcise demons and heal the paralyzed and lame (Acts 8:7). He may or may not have understood Philip's power to perform miracles and signs did not come from the same source as his sorcery. Either way, he thought he could buy it, much like he probably bought training and scrolls on sorcery. The Holy Spirit's power does not come through rituals or enchantments; it comes through believers aligning themselves with God's will and the Holy Spirit working through them. Simon was corrected for this misstep in very harsh terms and Simon did not want the judgment he had incurred (Acts 8:20-24).

As a side note, there are many who interpret Simon's faith as being false or spurious because he tried to buy the Holy Spirit's power. The passage does not indicate this; Simon believed, as it says in verse 13, and then he sinned. He reverted to his old way of thinking about sorcery and instead of learning more about the Holy Spirit's power, he tried to buy it. Just because he sinned and Peter pronounced judgment on the sin does not mean he didn't believe. He may have a lack of reward because of his sin, but he will be there (I Corinthians 3:15).

Acts 13:6-12 records an interaction Paul had with a sorcerer named Bar-Jesus or Elymas. Elymas was a Jew who is described as a sorcerer and false prophet, which shows the practices of magic and divination can be done by the same person. We aren't told of any signs Elymas did, but we do know he withstood Paul and Barnabas "seeking to turn the proconsul away from the faith" (Acts 13:8). Paul said to him, "O full of all deceit and all fraud, you son of the devil, you enemy of all righteousness, will you not cease perverting the straight ways of the Lord?" (Acts 8:10). Since Elymas was a Jew, he probably performed signs and gave prophecies claiming they were from the Hebrew God, but he was a fraud which Paul points out. He is exactly the kind of person the Old Testament pronounced such strong judgment against when talking about witchcraft and the diviners. Elymas is struck blind by Paul immediately after these words (Acts 13:11).

"Then the proconsul believed, when he saw what had been done, being astonished at the teaching of the Lord" (Act 13:12). The passage does not elaborate on what Paul and Barnabas were teaching, but since there was this interaction between them and Elymas, there must have been some information on why his sorcery and false prophecies were wrong in God's eyes. Not only did the proconsul hear doctrine, but there was a very real display of God's power in superiority over Elymas' ability. These things in conjunction gave the proconsul everything he needed to believe in Jesus as his Savior (I Thessalonians 1:5) instead of believing in Elymas' works and doctrine. We should learn from this story that we do not need to "get along" with sorcery and false prophecies when preaching God's Word. They are to be addressed and exposed for perverting the ways of God, and through that teaching people can believe.

When Paul went to Ephesus he had a very effective ministry "and many who had believed came confessing and telling their deeds. Also, many of those who had practiced magic brought their books together and burned them in the sight of all. And they counted up the value of them, and it totaled fifty thousand pieces of silver" (Acts 19:18-19). In one way or another, Paul communicated God's truth so that the new believers gave up their magic practices. This should tell us that we should give up any magic practices in which we are involved.

We also learn from this passage magic can be taught through books. The Bible doesn't state the content of the scrolls which were burned, but modern magic books contain rituals that supposedly allow you to control the elements, such as wind, water, or even solid objects. The further a book dives into the subject of magic the more talk there is of using a spiritual or non-physical world/plane to control the physical world. These magic books sometimes mention contacting "spirit lifeforms" in

Magic, Sorcery, and Witchcraft

order to assist a person in their spells. If the Bible is true, and it is, then any ability to control nature or matter outside of what is possible by normal human means has to be the work of demons.

These new believers in Ephesus gave up these practices and destroyed the books which explained magic practices. What happened after they did this? "So the word of the Lord grew mightily and prevailed" (Acts 19:20). I would not say the word of the Lord grew only because they burned their magic books; however, we can safely assume this was part of why it grew.

In the previous New Testament passages, the Greek words translated "sorcery" or "magic" mean "magic or curious arts." When we come to the Epistles and Revelation, the word translated "sorcery" changes to a form of the root word *pharmakon* where we get our English words "pharmaceutical" and "pharmacy." *Pharmekeia*, *pharmakeus*, and *pharmakos* are the other forms of the word used in the Bible. Before we look at the five verses where this word is used, we will look at different views of what this word might mean.

Pharmakon and its other forms can have many meanings just like our English word "drug." It can mean a medicine made from different ingredients used to heal an ailment. Conversely, it can mean a poison used to harm or kill something or someone. *Pharmekon* is also associated with potions used to manipulate a person's abilities, alter reality in a physical way, or as part of a magic ritual. In Greek mythology, it can be used as a synonym for *mageuo*, the Greek word most closely associated with our English word "magic" or "magick." With this wide range of meanings, context must determine meaning just like any other word.

In the Septuagint, a form of *pharmakon* is used to refer to divination and soothsaying as well as sorcery. Example verses of each of these uses are Isaiah 47:9, Jeremiah 27:9, and Micah 5:12.

This shows that before the New Testament was written, *pharmakon* had a wide range of meanings all connected with different forms of demonic power.

In the New Testament, each form of *pharmakon* is used in the following verses: *pharmakeia* (Galatians 5:20, Revelation 9:21, 18:23), *pharmakeus* (Revelation 21:8), *pharmakos* (Revelation 22:15). Except for Revelation 18:23, the word is used in a list of other sins with which unbelievers are associated. From the context, the meaning of *pharmakon* cannot be referring to a medicine or healing drug. However, the exact meaning—a poison, a potion associated with magic, or as a synonym for magic —is not clear.

Revelation 18:23 is talking about end times Babylon which will be an actually city, probably rebuilt at the same location as ancient Babylon. It says of the city, "For your merchants were the great men of the earth, for by your *pharmekeia* all the nations were deceived" (Revelation 18:23). Like the other passages, it is certain a positive or healing *pharmekeia* is not the meaning of the word in this verse. Other sins Babylon commits throughout Revelation 17 and 18 are fornication, blasphemy, abominations, harlotry, and the blood/killing of the saints. What is *pharmekeia* in this verse referring to? Poison? Negative drugs? Potions associated with magic? Magic? It is not clear, but whatever *pharmekeia* is, it is certainly important to the deception permeating the world during the Tribulation.

Christian theologians differ widely on what *pharmekeia* and its forms could mean. Especially in the early 2020's, *pharmekeia* received a lot of attention because the pharmaceutical industry exerted control over the events of the world. While we were given a glimpse of how drugs could be used during the Tribulation, we should not read this event into Revelation's use of *pharmekeia*. There is still not enough context to determine the exact meaning of John's use of the word, whether just a drug,

Magic, Sorcery, and Witchcraft

a drug with spiritual connections, or sorcery.

To give another view of *pharmekeia* and its meaning, modern witches and neo-pagans more often associate *pharmekeia* with magic, spells, and rituals. They look to Greek myths such as Medea and Kirke/Circe and how *pharmekeia* is used in those stories. In these Greek myths, *pharmekeia* can be a medicine, poison, a magic potion, or magic. When used in the context of a magic potion, there are sometimes even ingredient lists. There are many concoctions used in these stories to make a potion to aid a person in manipulating reality or to enter an altered state of consciousness. Could these things, reality manipulation or consciousness altering potions/drugs, be what Paul and John were referring to when they used *pharmekeia* and its forms? It is possible, but again there is not enough context to determine this.

In this chapter, we have talked about magic/sorcery, the calling of demons to manipulate creation. With this information, we should be able to notice all the ways demons can alter reality as we grow closer to the Tribulation.

Chapter 23

Mediums, Spiritists, Necromancy, and Familiar Spirits

With the previous two practices, divination and magic, humans attempt to contact demons through rituals to get them to reveal information or manipulate matter. Mediums and spiritists are also contacting demons, also called familiar spirits, but the demon is given a more prominent role. The demon still gives out information, but it is not necessarily focused on the future.

The first mention of mediums and familiar spirits is Leviticus 19:31 where God says very pointedly, "Give no regard to mediums and familiar spirits; do not seek after them, to be defiled by them: I am the LORD your God." There is no reason to contact another spiritual source of knowledge; God is everything an Israelite or any believer needs. In fact, the judgment is given in Leviticus 20:6: "And the person who turns to mediums and familiar spirits, to prostitute himself with them, I will set My face against that person and cut him off from his people." God likens contacting demons to prostitution, indicating a form of "spiritual adultery" we are committing against God.

God knew there would be people who try to contact

demons, so He told Israel, "A man or a woman who is a medium, or who has familiar spirits, shall surely be put to death; they shall stone them with stones. Their blood shall be upon them" (Leviticus 20:27). This verse also gives us the definition of a medium, that it is a man or woman who is familiar with a spirit. They are in contact with the spirit and use the demon to lead people away from God, either knowingly or unknowingly. God gave the command to Israel to put them to death, not the Church; we do not execute mediums or spiritists in our age. However, we should still follow the principle of not being involved with them.

The most detailed account of a medium and their familiar spirit is the account of king Saul seeking out the medium at En Dor in I Samuel 28:3-25. Saul had begun his reign well in this area, by putting the mediums and spiritists out of the land just as Leviticus 20:27 says. However, Saul had grown apart from God so far that God would not answer his inquiries. When God did not answer, Saul instead sought a medium in order to ask the deceased Samuel what to do. Saul's goal was to contact the dead, a practice known as necromancy, in order to know the future. Looking at this idea at face value, why would a dead person have any insight into the future?

Even though the medium must have hidden her practice to avoid death, she was known enough for his soldiers to find her. Saul asks her, "Please conduct a séance for me, and bring up for me the one I shall name to you" (I Samuel 28:9). The medium knows that her practice would earn her death, but Saul assures her she will not die.

> Then the woman said, "Whom shall I bring up for you?" And he said, "Bring up Samuel for me." When the woman saw Samuel, she cried out with a loud voice. And the woman spoke to Saul, saying, "Why have you

Mediums, Spiritists, Necromancy, and Familiar Spirits

deceived me? For you are Saul!" And the king said to her, "Do not be afraid. What did you see?" And the woman said to Saul, "I saw a spirit ascending out of the earth." So he said to her, "What is his form?" And she said, "An old man is coming up and he is covered with a mantle." And Saul perceived that it was Samuel, and he stooped with his face to the ground and bowed down.
I Samuel 28:11-14

Why did the woman cry out when she saw Samuel? Because she was not expecting his form but something else. Since she was a medium, she was expecting the spirit(s) she worked with to appear. But instead the form of a man appeared. God intervened when the medium was counting on her familiar spirit to appear.

God had already condemned the practice of contacting spirits (Leviticus 19:31) and one who calls up the dead (Deuteronomy 18:11) in the Mosiac law. But in this instance, He allowed a dead Samuel to be contacted. Why did God do this? We aren't given a direct reason, but we do know the only message Samuel had for Saul was one of judgment and death. We should not take this story as precedent for trying to contact anyone from the dead through a medium lest we be judged also.

Isaiah gives the admonition, "And when they say to you, 'Seek those who are mediums and wizards, who whisper and mutter,' should not a people seek their God? Should they seek the dead on behalf of the living?" (Isaiah 8:19). Jerusalem, in one of the passages about God's judgment, is likened to a medium's voice: "You shall be brought down, you shall speak out of the ground; your speech shall be low, out of the dust; you voice shall be like a medium's, out of the ground; and your speech shall whisper out of the dust" (Isaiah 29:4). God even judges pagan nations because of mediums, saying to Egypt, "'The spirit of

Deceiving by Signs

Egypt will fail in its midst; I will destroy their counsel, and they will consult the idols and the charmers, the mediums and the sorcerers. And the Egyptians I will give into the hand of a cruel master, and a fierce king will rule over them,' says the Lord, the LORD of Hosts" (Isaiah 19:3-4).

There is no New Testament verse directly addressing mediums, familiar spirits, or necromancy, which leads us to believe God has not changed His opinion about getting involved in this practice. These practices are still very common today, and we would do well to avoid them.

Chapter 24

Astrology

The practice of astrology, either worshiping celestial objects or tracking their movements to gain knowledge, is not mentioned often in the Bible but is worth mentioning as a demonic power. The same magicians, sorcerers, diviners, and wise men we have talked about in other chapters were also involved in astrology or may have been the practice to which they were devoted. Demons can certainly be involved in Astrology as a method of divination.

Deuteronomy 4:19 says, "And take heed, lest you lift your eyes to heaven, and when you see the sun, the moon, and the stars, all the host of heaven, you feel driven to worship them and serve them, which the LORD your God has given to all the people under the whole heaven as a heritage." This passage is in the context of Moses warning the Israelites to not fall into idolatry. The Egyptians were involved in the worship of celestial objects, so it would be natural for the Israelites to be drawn to this practice since they would have been familiar with it.

The host of heaven were created by God "to divide the day from the night; and let them be for signs and seasons, and for days and years; and let them be for lights in the firmament of the heavens to give light on the earth" (Genesis 1:14-15) as well as "to rule over the day and over the night, and to divide the light from the darkness" (Genesis 1:18). The heavens are also often used by God to declare His glory (Psalm 19:1) or His invisible attributes (Romans 1:20). But never are we to worship them nor anything created.

God challenged the Babylonians' practice of astrology to save them from His judgment:

> Stand now with your enchantments and the multitude of your sorceries, in which you have labored from your youth — perhaps you will be able to profit, perhaps you will prevail. You are wearied in the multitude of your counsels; let now the astrologers, the stargazers, and the monthly prognosticators stand up and save you from what shall come upon you. Behold, they shall be as stubble, the fire shall burn them; they shall not deliver themselves from the power of the flame; it shall not be a coal to be warmed by, nor a fire to sit before! Thus shall they be to you with whom you have labored, your merchants from your youth; they shall wander each one to his quarter. No one shall save you.
> *Isaiah 47:12-15*

The astrologers of Babylon certainly would not predict disaster upon Babylon; if they did, they may have been killed by the king. Astrology was only accurate enough to be ten times worse than Daniel (Daniel 1:20), but even with some measure of success those predictions would have no power over God's judgment upon them.

In the New Testament, the magi/wise men who visited Jesus were watching the stars in anticipation of the birth of the King of the Jews (Matthew 2:1-2). What part of the east did they come from and how did they know about the Messiah's birth? First and foremost, they had to have copies of the Jewish Scriptures to study. The most likely location from the east where Jews resided and the Scriptures were brought is Babylon where Daniel gave his seventy weeks prophecy (Daniel 9:24-27). If they were from Babylon, these wise men held the same office as Daniel, which means they studied astrology (Daniel 1:5, 20).

A star announcing the birth of the Messiah is mentioned by Balaam in Numbers 24:17: "I see Him, but not now; I behold Him, but not near; a Star shall come out of Jacob; A Scepter shall rise out of Israel, and batter the brow of Moab, and destroy all the sons of tumult." This prophecy must have been available to the magi in Babylon and they had been taught the link between this prophecy and Daniel's prophecies. What they lacked was Micah 5:2, with documents the location of the Messiah's birth as Bethlehem.

God was using their practice of astrology to get them to travel to Israel just like He used divination to move Nebuchadnezzar to attack Jerusalem (Ezekiel 21:19-23). God is not affirming these practices but using them in the absence of Godly ones to accomplish His will. By following the star, which apparently appeared when Jesus was born (Matthew 2:7), the wise men were not lead to the Messiah but Herod. The magi were faithful, but lacked knowledge in their walk with God. These men were most likely saved because the focus of their journey was to worship the King (Matthew 2:2, 11). God also protected them by warning them "they should not return to Herod" (Matthew 2:12). Did these men continue in astrology when they returned to their own country? Probably, but in the presence of the Creator of the stars they followed Him rather than His creation.

Before leaving this story, what exactly was the star the magi followed? The star appeared, meaning it was not visible before

Jesus was born. Theoretically a physical star could have started nuclear fusion at the time of Jesus' birth. However, the star moves after the magi talked with Herod and stood where Jesus was (Matthew 2:9). Clearly, this was not a normal star but something God was doing supernaturally. The wise men realized the significance of this and "rejoiced with exceedingly great joy" (Matthew 2:10). This "star" was very different from other stars they studied and I think they knew it. Like the magicians in Egypt who recognized the "finger of God" (Exodus 8:19), these astrologers knew when a God greater than the gods they worshiped performed miracles. Even though astrology can get things right occasionally, God is always superior in His power if we are willing to notice the difference.

Chapter 25

Demon Possession

Interestingly, the Bible does not mention demons possessing humans until the Gospels, yet the Jews are able to identify when a human has a demon inside them (Mark 9:17), which indicates it happened before Jesus started His ministry. In the Gospels, there are various signs indicating the presence of an unclean spirit in a person. In this chapter, we will look at how a demon may enter a person, what happens while they are in the body, how do they leave, and what happens after they are gone. Along the way we'll even see other creatures demons are able to possess.

We are never told specifically how a demon gets inside a person. The only account in the Bible of a spirit entering a person is Satan entering Judas in John 13:27 and Luke 22:3. In both passages, it simply says Satan entered Judas. As we discussed before, Judas was not a believer (John 6:64), he already had wicked desires (John 12:6), and Satan had already been negatively influencing his thoughts (John 13:2). Other than those things, we are left to speculate how and why Satan entered Judas' body.

Did he have to receive permission for God to enter Judas? Did Judas give him permission? Was Judas' propensity for evil enough that Satan was able to enter him without any permission? We don't know the answers to any of these questions.

If we speculate, demon possession may follow the same pattern as other demonic contact: first, there is some sort of ritual or act performed, then the demon performs a sign or wonder or in this case possessing a person. I believe this is the closest we can get to an explanation, although I will repeat this is speculation. Any other details about how possession happens can't be answered authoritatively because the Bible does not give us more detail.

Leaving how exactly possession happens, we know possession can happen at different ages. The Bible mentions sons and daughters being possessed (Matthew 15:22, Mark 9:17) although we don't know their exact ages. Other possessions mentioned must be adults with different ages throughout adulthood. The Bible also records both men and women being possessed (Matthew 9:32, 15:22). We also know more than one demon can inhabit a body (Matthew 12:45 , Mark 5:9, Luke 8:2).

We aren't told in any case other than Judas whether a person who was possessed was a believer. In the church age when someone believes in Jesus, the Holy Spirit immediately indwells them (I Corinthians 6:19) and since Christ has no fellowship with Belial (II Corinthians 6:15), we are safe to say church age believers cannot be possessed by demons. However, in the Old Testament, the Holy Spirit did not indwell all believers. In fact, David specifically said, "Do not take Your Holy Spirit from me" (Psalm 51:11). Does this mean believers before the church age could be indwelt by demons? Possibly, but the Bible does not say one way or the other. But for our time and most likely in all ages no believer can be possessed.

One other question to answer about how a person can be

possessed is how often it happens to people across the globe. Jesus encounters both Jews and Gentiles who are demon possessed, so theoretically all nationalities of people can be possessed. The Gospels mention demon possession quite a bit, and there are a few references in Acts, but throughout the rest of the Bible there is no mention of possession. If the Jews were able to identify when a person is possessed, theoretically it must have happened in the Old Testament, although we have no idea how often. Since possession happens in Acts, we know it is possible during the church age, but again we have no idea of frequency. Possession may happen more frequently in places demon congregate (Revelation 18:2) which has to do with the amount of evil present in any given location. Even though there is a lot of detail about possession we may want to know, the Bible is silent on many of these issues. God always tells us to stay away from practices involving demon contact, so it is probably best to avoid anything to do with possession unless God specifically puts it in your path to deal with.

Once a demon or demons enter a person, various things happen as the demons manifest their power. We know from Luke 11:26 and Matthew 12:45 there are varying degrees of wickedness among demons for it says "Other spirits more wicked than himself." Therefore the various things that happen to a person when they are possessed most likely depends on the wickedness and quantity of the demons present in the body. It is also worth noting there are many diseases and physical conditions mentioned alongside the effects of demon possession, so we know some illnesses and infirmities can be caused by demons.

It seems there are two basic ways a demon impacts the person they possess: one is to make their body not work correctly in different ways and the other is to exaggerate the abilities of a person's body. In each case, the person is tormented by the demon(s). There is no "fun" aspect of demon possession nor does the demon turn them into a type of super hero. Jesus says when an unclean spirit leaves a man, the man he left becomes "swept and put in order" (Luke 11:25). This indicates possession wrecks havoc on a person's life and when they leave there is the ability to clean it up. There is no positive light ever placed on demon possession in the Bible.

Luke 6:18 says Jesus healed "those who were tormented with unclean spirits." How were they tormented? One way a demon can cause suffering is to make a person mute. Matthew 9:32-34 tells of a man who was demon possessed and mute. Once Jesus cast out the demon, the man was able to speak. Not only can a demon make a person mute, but also blind as Matthew 12:22 records. Jesus also healed this man and he was able to speak and see. In Matthew 15:22, a woman says her daughter is "severely demon possessed" although we are not given symptoms other than she was healed (Matthew 15:28). Another person Jesus healed was a woman who had a spirit of infirmity for eighteen years which caused her to be bent over so that she could not raise herself up (Luke 13:11), which means the demon manipulated her skeletal structure. The man possessed by Legion was "crying out and cutting himself with stones" (Mark 5:5). The demons seem to cause mentally instability as well as the person inflicting self harm. This man also wore no clothes (Luke 8:27) although we aren't told the reason for this.

Matthew, Mark, and Luke each record the account of a man's son who "is an epileptic and suffers severely; for he often falls into the fire and often into the water" (Matthew 17:15). Jesus calls this spirit a "deaf and dumb spirit," (Mark 9:25), and Mark records the father telling Jesus, "Wherever it seizes him, it throws him down; he foams at the mouth, gnashes his teeth, and becomes rigid" (Mark 9:18). Luke further elaborates: "He suddenly cries out; it convulses him so that he foams at the mouth; and it departs from him with great difficulty, bruising him" (Luke 9:39). When the boy saw Jesus, "Immediately the spirit convulsed him, and he fell on the ground and wallowed, foaming at the mouth" (Mark 9:20). This account shows demons can have quite a bit of control over a person's body. The demon threw the boy around and made the body react with fluids.

Moving to what happens when a demon exaggerates the abilities of a person, the story of the two demon possessed men in Gergesenes says the men were "exceedingly fierce, so that no one could pass that way" (Matthew 8:28). They were also living around tombs (Matthew 8:28) just like the man possessed with Legion (Mark 5:5). Demons may influence people to be around places of death or where there are more demons, but we shouldn't build a doctrine off small statements without much detail. Mark also mentions the man possessed by Legion was living in the mountains (Mark 5:5) and Luke says the demon drove him into the wilderness (Luke 8:29), making it clear demons do have some amount of control over where a person goes.

Speaking of Legion in Mark 5:1-20, the demons in this man made him very strong for he was able to break chains. The demon possessed man in Acts 19:13-16 also is indicated to be very strong because he was able to overpower seven men, leaving them wounded and naked. No one could tame Legion, which sounds like the "exceedingly fierce" men from Gergesenes (Matthew 8:28). Luke mentions the man had demons for a long time (Luke 8:27), so it may be the control a demon has over a person is related to not only the number and wickedness of the demon(s) present, but also the time they have spent in the person. The boy in Mark 9:17-29 is said to have had his condition from childhood, which indicates some time had passed since the first time his condition manifested.

Demons seem to be able to come and go from people they have possessed, although it is hard to tell when or why this happens. Satan entered Judas twice (Luke 22:3, John 13:27) which means he had to leave once. The man's son who had a demon in Mark 9:18 said, "whenever it seizes him." This may indicate the demon would leave and come back, but it also may indicate the demon choose to effect the boy at some times and not others. When Jesus rebuked the demon, He told him to "Come out of him and enter him no more!" (Mark 9:25). Maybe the spirit entered the boy multiple times and was not allowed to enter him ever again, or it could just mean the demon wasn't allowed to enter any more.

Jesus tells us about a situation in which a demon leaves a person in Luke and Matthew 12:43-45:

> When an unclean spirit goes out of a man, he goes through dry places, seeking rest; and finding none, he says, "I will return to my house from which I came." And when he comes, he finds it swept and put in order. Then he goes and takes with him seven other spirits more wicked than himself, and they enter and dwell there; and the last state of that man is worse than the first.
> *Luke 11:24-26*

Jesus doesn't say under what circumstances a demon does this, so this situation could happen when a demon is exorcised or when the demon leaves the body for whatever reason. It may be the demon leaves a person of his own free will, or there is some other reason the demon leaves. We do know the demon is able to enter the body again, and not only that but able to bring more demons into the body with him. Whatever circumstances lead to the demon going out of a man, when the demon returns the man is far worse off because now more demons are present.

Jesus mentions the unclean spirit going through "dry places" before returning to the man. It is difficult to know what is meant by this because demons travel unseen by us. A "dry place" could mean the demon found nothing to do any place he went. Since the demon left a person, he may be seeking another person to possess. We don't know how much autonomy demons have apart from Satan's directives, so its hard to say what demons do when they are not inside a person. But in some way, he decides to return to the person he used to possess

Where are the "places" the demon goes through? We know demons do not dwell in heaven anymore (Job 1:6) but we also know they have access to heaven (1 Kings 22:19-22). Therefore, demons must dwell in our universe somewhere. Since demons are ruled by Satan (Revelation 12:7) and his goals revolve around ruling earth (Isaiah 14:13-14), they are probably "going to and fro on the earth, and from walking back and forth on it" (Job 1:7) just like Satan. Using this logic, the "places" demons go are probably anywhere over the surface of the earth at any altitude they want.

What "rest" is the demon seeking? The Bible talks a lot about peace and rest being in Jesus Christ (John 14:27, Hebrews 4:11); since demons have no opportunity for a restful relationship with Jesus, maybe there is no rest for them. They could be in a constant state of torture if the "dryness" of their journey gives them nothing to contemplate except their own judgment (Matthew 8:29, 25:41). If they are possessing a person, maybe that eases their thoughts enough because it gives them something else to focus on. This is speculation on the psychology of a demon, about which the Bible does not give us much information, but in some way the demon is restless and is looking for something to do.

If we explore this passage a bit further, where did the demon find the "seven other spirits more wicked than himself?" Were they also going through "dry places?" Were they occupied with another task and decided possessing someone was better than what they were already doing? Arguably this passage has more questions than answers, but we know demon possession isn't good the first time and gets worse if it happens again.

Demons can be cast out of a person by either Jesus Himself or believers. Jesus always cast out demons with words and they obeyed Him. When Jesus casts out a demon, He often says, "Come out of him," sometimes adding a rebuke or other instructions (Mark 1:25, 5:8, 9:25). Paul used the same pattern when he cast the demon out of the possessed girl in Acts 16:18 saying, "I command you in the name of Jesus Christ to come out of her." Jesus is God and His power to tell demons what to do is not limited, but humans must appropriate His name to do the same thing. Jesus' Name has power, and when applied correctly, demons cannot resist it. The Jewish exorcists in Acts 19:13-16 did not understand Jesus' power but rather said, "We exorcise you by the Jesus whom Paul preaches." These men are not said to be believers, and this statement sounds as if they are trying to appropriate Paul's method of exorcism rather than understand why it worked. The demon the men were trying to exorcise did not leave the man, and the exorcists were beaten as a consequence.

Jesus said to the father of a demon possessed boy, "If you can believe, all things are possible to him who believes" (Mark 9:23). The father, with tears in his eyes, cried out, "Lord, I believe; help my unbelief!" (Mark 9:24). Jesus, Who does not need to call on His own name, rebuked the unclean spirit and commanded him to come out of the boy (Mark 9:25). Using Jesus' Name to command demons only works when there is faith in Him and His ability. A demon will not listen to someone who merely says the Name of Jesus, but they will listen to someone who trusts that Jesus will accomplish the task through His power and not our own. Anyone's ability to cast out demons is dependent on their faith, and then Jesus will accomplish the task.

In another story in Mark, there was a person casting out demons who was not one of the twelve disciples (Mark 9:38). The disciples told him to stop, "But Jesus said, 'Do not forbid him, for no one who works a miracle in My name can soon afterward speak evil of Me. For he who is not against us is on our side'" (Mark 9:39-40). The faithful person, even though he was not necessarily told he could cast out demons, appropriated the power of Jesus' Name to cast them out.

After the demon leaves the possessed boy of the father in Mark 9:17-29, Jesus' disciples asked "Him privately, 'Why could we not cast it out?' So He said to them, 'This kind can come out by nothing but prayer and fasting'" (Mark 9:28-29). Apparently there are demons or groups of demons too powerful for believers to command them to come out. It takes prayer and fasting, presumably over a period of time, in order to get them to leave the person. This boy was a severe case of possession, and the demons had probably been there for a while. These may be the circumstances under which fasting and prayer is required. Fasting and prayer are ways of submitting ourselves to God, so even though an exorcism may take more than our words, Jesus' ability is still the only power to make demons leave someone. No rituals of any other kind are ever mentioned in connection with exorcisms, so we should be wary of any practices of casting out demons going beyond words in Jesus' Name, fasting, and prayer.

Distance may not be a factor when casting out demons. Jesus was able to heal the woman's daughter when the girl was not there (Matthew 15:28). There are also cases of Jesus healing sicknesses from a distance, such as centurion's servant in Matthew 8:5-13. It is more common for the person being healed of demon possession or sickness to be present with the person doing the healing, but if the healing is based on God's power,

God can heal anyone anywhere. Any healing is done by God's ability alone, and while we are restricted by space, God is not.

When Jesus sent out the twelve disciples in Luke 9, He "gave them power and authority over all demons" (Luke 9:1). The disciples used this power and authority and "cast out many demons" (Mark 6:13). The seventy disciples Jesus sent out were also able to cast out demons in Jesus' name (Luke 10:17). This may have been a special authority Jesus gave to the disciples before the church age because in Acts the apostles, Philip, and Paul were all able to cast out unclean spirits without being given special authority (Acts 5:16, 8:7, 16:18, 19:12). Each of the people able to cast out demons in Acts had great faith and were used mightily by God. This may indicate only believers who are very strong in faith are able to cast out demons or called to do so, but there are no parameters around who is able or not. Any believer may be able to perform an exorcism, but it is probably best to only get involved if you are a mature believer.

In some cases before demons leave the body, they communicated with Jesus. The demon possessed man in the synagogue in Capernaum cried out, "Let us alone! What have we to do with You, Jesus of Nazareth? Did You come to destroy us? I know who You are—the Holy One of God!" (Mark 1:24). Legion "cried out with a loud voice and said, 'What have I to do with You, Jesus, Son of the Most High God? I implore You by God that you do not torment me'" (Mark 5:7). Both demons want to be left alone, presumably to go about their life without Jesus' intervention. They also know exactly Who Jesus' is. Legion even appeals to God for Jesus to leave him alone. There are many reasons the demons could have said these things to Jesus; maybe they deceived themselves into thinking they can possess people without consequences or want to avoid what is coming when Jesus encounters them. Whatever the reason, demons possessing people do not want to be evicted by Jesus' power.

Demon Possession

Demons also bartered with Jesus about what will happen after they are exorcised. The demons in the two men at Gergesenes and Legion both ask Jesus if they can inhabit a herd of pigs (Matthew 8:31, Mark 5:12). In both cases, when the demons enter the swine the whole herd dies by running into the sea. There is much speculation on why this happened, but the Bible doesn't tell us the reason. Even though demons are able to enter animals, we don't know if it is common or anything about how an animal will act under the influence of a demon other than these pigs that immediately died.

When a demon finally does leave, the body can physically react to the demon's departure. In the case of the father's son who was demon possessed, Mark says, "The spirit cried out, convulsed him greatly, and came out of him. And he became as one dead, so that many said, 'He is dead'" (Mark 9:26). Other times, it seems the demons leave peacefully, such as Legion in which is simply states, "Then the unclean spirits went out" (Mark 5:13).

After a demon leaves, the person is always completely healed of whatever effects the demon had on them. Most of the time we are not given the story of what happens in a person's life after the demon is cast out. A person does not necessarily place their faith in Jesus as their Savior immediately after their healing, and when this doesn't happen the demon may be able to return (Luke 11:24-26). But sometimes the person not only becomes a believer, but a disciple as well. The man possessed with Legion begged Jesus that he might follow Him, but Jesus did not allow it, instead giving him a job as an evangelist: "'Go home to your friends, and tell them what great things the Lord has done for you, and how He has had compassion on you.' And he departed and began to proclaim in Decapolis all that Jesus had done for him; and all marveled" (Mark 5:19-20). An attitude of deep devotion, thankfulness, and an excitement to tell others about Jesus is the proper response to any healing of demon possession.

Chapter 26

Doctrine of Demons

The Bible does not mention deception in conjunction with demons' powers very often. However, the common theme throughout all their abilities is to deceive people into not following God's way and believing a lie. One of the most powerful abilities of demons is to teach doctrine opposite God's. Paul says to Timothy, "Now the Spirit expressly says that in the latter times some will depart from the faith, giving heed to deceiving spirits and doctrines of demons" (I Timothy 4:1).

Immediately after saying this, Paul gives Timothy a few examples of demonic doctrine: "Speaking lies in hypocrisy… forbidding to marry, and commanding to abstain from foods which God created to be received with thanksgiving by those who believe and know the truth." (I Timothy 4:2-3). Earlier in the letter Paul says, "Charge some that they teach no other doctrine, nor give heed to fables and endless genealogies, which cause disputes rather than godly edification which is in faith" (I Timothy 1:3-4). Other examples of false doctrine in I Timothy include profane and old wives' fables, unwholesome words not in accord with godliness, disputes and arguments over words, desiring to be rich, profane and idle babblings, and contradictions of what is falsely called knowledge (I Timothy 4:7, 6:3, 6:4, 6:9, 6:20).

While Paul gave some examples of demonic doctrine that are still around today, James gives us the qualities of their wisdom: "But if you have bitter envy and self-seeking in your hearts, do not boast and lie against the truth. This wisdom does not descend from above, but it earthly, sensual, demonic. For where envy and self-seeking exist, confusion and every evil thing are there" (James 3:14-16). When a person is teaching or expressing their thoughts, if envy, self-seeking, and confusion are in their words, that wisdom is opposite God's. That does not necessarily mean demons directly contact them and taught them their wisdom, but rather the source of the wisdom is demons rather than God.

Paul warns the Colossians, "Beware lest anyone cheat you through philosophy and empty deceit, according to the tradition of men, according to the basic principles of the world, and not according to Christ" (Colossians 2:8). The basic principles of the world are leaving God out of explanations for creation or anything else that happens. It is interesting that on one hand so many of demons' powers are focused on getting people to believe in supernatural or spiritual things apart from God, yet on the other hand demons through men will teach there is no God.

James told us what Godly wisdom isn't, then he tells us what Godly wisdom is: "But the wisdom that is from above is first pure, then peaceable, gentle, willing to yield, full of mercy and good fruits, without partiality and without hypocrisy. Now the fruit of righteousness is sown in peace by those who make peace" (James 3:17-18). Believers' doctrine should be striving for peace, but that does not mean we never say anything that makes people uncomfortable. Rather, it is the opposite of envy and self-seeking which is what demons preach.

Doctrine of Demons

In Ephesians 5:11, Paul says, "And have no fellowship with the unfruitful works of darkness, but rather expose them." When you expose works and doctrine people believe that do not come from God, it can make people uncomfortable or even enrage them. How do we do this if we are to make peace? The peace we are to sow is God's peace, "which surpasses all understanding," and "will guard your hearts and minds through Christ Jesus" (Philippians 4:7). God's peace often comes with a battle upfront, for Jesus Himself even said, "Do not think that I came to bring peace on earth. I did not come to bring peace but a sword" (Matthew 10:34). The "sword" is God's Word, exposing our need for a Savior and dividing even families over whether we believe God's Word or not (Matthew 10:35-37). Once we believe the Gospel, then choose to follow God's commands as disciples by taking up our cross and losing our life (Matthew 10:38-39), we are given Jesus' peace, even though we are divided from unbelievers. His peace is not as the world, demons included, gives peace, but a peace through the tribulations we will encounter for our faith. "In the world you will have tribulation; but be of good cheer, I have overcome the world" (John 16:33).

There is no peace in our lives when we seek it from the world. Jesus has already overcome the world, and "in Him dwells all the fullness of the Godhead bodily; and you are complete in Him, who is the head of all principality and power" (Colossians 2:9-10). Jesus rules the unclean spirits, therefore His knowledge and ability make us complete without seeking other sources of peace. When we depend on Him for everything through our tribulation, we truly will have a peace that surpasses understanding.

Chapter 27

Judgment for Abominations in the Old Testament

As we have talked about demonic power, it is clear many of the powers overlap or often work with each other. For example, divination is connected with curses because both deal with the future. Often the same people who participate in divination practices perform magic. This chapter will mention some of the verses that include other rituals used in connection with demons' power.

God said to the children of Israel,

> When you come into the land which the LORD your God is giving you, you shall not learn to follow the abominations of those nations. There shall not be found among you anyone who makes his son or his daughter pass through the fire, or one who practices witchcraft, or a soothsayer, or one who interprets omens, or a sorcerer, or one who conjures spells, or a medium, or a spiritist, or one who calls up the dead. For all who do these things are an abomination to the LORD, and because of these abominations the LORD your God drives them out from before you. You shall be blameless before the

LORD your God. For these nations which you will dispossess listened to soothsayers and diviners; but as for you, the LORD your God has not appointed such for you.
Deuteronomy 18:9-14

We have talked about each of these nine things in previous chapters except for children passing through the fire. The Canaanite form of this practice was to place a baby in the arms of a heated metal idol to sacrifice the child to their gods. God told the Israelites specifically to not participate in this practice earlier in Leviticus 18:21: "And you shall not let any of your descendants pass through the fire to Molech."

Another thing about the Deuteronomy passage to note is the word "abominations" repeated three times. "Abominations of the nations" is a phrase repeated throughout Israel's history; for example: "They did according to all the abominations of the nations which the LORD had cast out before the children of Israel" (I Kings 14:24). There were other things God called an abomination, such as lying with a male as with a female (Leviticus 18:22), so it is not only these nine practices that are included in the abominations of the nations, but they certainly were detestable for God to specifically point them out.

In the Deuteronomy passage, God repeats Himself as "the LORD your God" four times. God is emphasizing, as He often does, He is God and the children of Israel belong to Him. Getting involved in rituals and practices to contact or worship demons is not how God wants us to act; He wants us to contact Him in faith and prayer for everything we need.

At the end of the northern kingdom of Israel, Manasseh's reign included passing his son through the fire, soothsaying, witchcraft, and consulting spiritists, and mediums (II Kings 21:6).

Judgment for Abominations in the Old Testament

God spoke by the prophets saying,

> Because Manasseh king of Judah has done these abominations (he has acted more wickedly than all the Amorites who were before him, and has also made Judah sin with his idols), therefore thus says the LORD God of Israel: "Behold, I am bringing such calamity upon Jerusalem and Judah, that whoever hears of it, both his ears with tingle."
> *II Kings 21:11-12*

Manasseh's sin, which included the abominations mentioned in Deuteronomy 18:9-14, was so bad that people's ears would tingle when hearing about it.

While these are Old Testament verses and we are in a different dispensation today, there is no indication of God reversing His position on whether contacting demons to use their powers or child sacrifice is an abomination. There is judgment for doing these things, and God will handle church age believer's sin either temporally or at the judgment seat of Christ (II Corinthians 5:9-11) rather than how He judged Israel.

Idolatry is another very large topic in the Bible, and worship of idols can be used to contact demons for their power even though that is not always the purpose. Not participating in idolatry is one of the ten commandments, which shows how important it is to God:

> You shall not make for yourself a carved image—any likeness of anything that is in heaven above, or that is in the earth beneath, or that is in the water under the earth; you shall not bow down to them nor serve them. For I, the LORD your God, am a jealous God, visiting the iniquity of the fathers upon the children to the third and fourth generations of those who hate Me, but showing

mercy to thousands, to those who love Me and keep My commandments.
Deuteronomy 5:8-10

God says there will be judgment for idolatry but mercy to those who do not participate in the practice. God has never changed His position on idolatry, for John ends one of his letters with "Little children, keep yourselves from idols" (I John 5:21).

Can demons communicate through or manipulate objects such as idols? The only direct reference to this happening is Revelation 13:15, in which the false prophet "was granted power to give breath to the image of the beast, that the image of the beast should both speak and cause as many as would not worship the image of the beast to be killed." Considering the image was made animate through the false prophet's power, this does not seem like a trick or something digital like a hologram, but an actual object that became a "living" and moving thing capable of killing those who do not worship it. If it is possible during the Tribulation to make idols speak and move, theoretically it is possible for demons to do this now.

Chapter 28

Demonic Power in the Eschaton

During the Tribulation, we are not given specifics for how demons' will manifest their power. Matthew 24:24 says, "For false christs and false prophets will rise and show great signs and wonders to deceive, if possible, even the elect." These false christs and prophets may not be unified in their message but could deceive people into believing in many different things other than Jesus. The false prophet will be the strongest of all these deceivers and will perform

> Great signs, so that he even makes fire come down from heaven on the earth in the sight of men. And he deceives those who dwell on the earth by those signs which he was granted to do in the sight of the beast, telling those who dwell on the earth to make an image to the beast who was wounded by the sword and lived. He was granted power to give breath to the image of the beast, that the image of the beast should both speak and cause as many as would not worship the image of the beast to be killed.
>
> *Revelation 13:13-15*

Deceiving by Signs

Satan may grant him the ability to make fire come from the sky and the other signs the false prophet does will deceive men into worship of the beast, culminating in the creation of the image. We saw the magicians in Egypt turn their staves into snakes, so giving an image breathe sounds like another form of this demonic power.

Later in John's vision, he

> Saw three unclean spirits like frogs coming out of the mouth of the dragon, out of the mouth of the beast, and out of the mouth of the false prophet. For they are spirits of demons, performing signs, which go out to the kings of the earth and of the whole world, to gather them to the battle of that great day of God Almighty.
> Revelation 16:13-14

This is the only verse saying spirits will perform signs without the need of a human mediator. This seems to be the epitome of power for demons in which their power is plainly seen and experienced throughout the world. All the powers we have mentioned so far—divination, magic, mediums and familiar spirits, astrology, possession—will most likely be very prevalent during the Tribulation.

This would be a natural consequence once the Restrainer, the Holy Spirit through the Church, is taken out of the way (II Thessalonians 2:7); there will be nothing to restrain the demons using their power however they choose. God will still be present and working through the 144,000 to get people saved, but the lack of restraint on Satan and his demons will embolden them throughout the Tribulation to use their power to deceive the world. People in the Tribulation will possibly see an even greater magnitude of the signs we've studied. These inferences are why I believe today we are seeing more and more signs from demons as we grow closer to the Rapture.

MODERN POWER, SIGNS, AND WONDERS

We have studied Satan and demons throughout the Bible, having seen who they are and their capabilities. This gives us the foundation we need to interpret signs and wonders we see in our modern day.

"Now the Spirit expressly says that in the latter times some will depart from the faith, giving heed to deceiving spirits and doctrines of demons" (I Timothy 4:1). Paul also says, "Evil men and impostors will grow worse and worse, deceiving and being deceived" (II Timothy 3:13). Putting these two verses together, demons will influence people with false doctrine; those that are deceived will grow more and more deceived, but also will be able to deceive others more easily. I think we can also put signs and wonders along with the demons' doctrine because signs are often a way to confirm a teaching. Signs will also be more prevalent in the Tribulation, and, just like other aspects of the Tribulation we see being prepared in our day, I believe we will see signs more frequently as the stage continues to be set for the Antichrist's rule.

This section is devoted to looking at power, signs, and

wonders we see right now and how these things are preparing the world for the signs they will see during the Tribulation. All these signs are aimed at deceiving people into believing lies and not God's truth; therefore anything supernatural or paranormal that does not draw people to God is a likely candidate for demonic power. This section is speculation, so obviously it does not have the authority the Bible has. It is also not an in depth look at each topic; we are only seeking to give an overview of modern ways Satan or demons could manifest their power and how to interpret signs through the lens of Scripture.

If you choose to research any of these topics further, make sure you are praying and rooted in Scripture before beginning. My wife and I have experienced what we can only interpret as demonic influence while we have researched some of these subjects. It is very important to have a firm grasp of Scripture because the viewpoints the signs are attempting to confirm are very attractive to our human mind. We can be swayed very easily into believing non-Biblical ideas through getting involved in paranormal and supernatural activity, so make sure you are spiritually ready before any research endeavor.

There are two main tests through which we will run each sign. One is from Deuteronomy 13:2, in which a sign or wonder either leads us to worship God or not. The other is from I John:

> Beloved, do not believe every spirit, but test the spirits, whether they are of God; because many false prophets have gone out in the world. By this you know the Spirit of God: Every spirit that confesses that Jesus Christ has come in the flesh is of God, and every spirit that does not confess that Jesus Christ has come in the flesh is not of God. And this is the spirit of the Antichrist, which you have heard was coming, and is now already in the world.
> *I John 4:1-3*

Modern Power, Signs, and Wonders

Any spirit or entity that disperses knowledge should be asked what they think of Jesus of Nazareth. If this spirit does not confess Jesus as coming in the flesh, they are a deceiving spirit and attempting to prepare us to follow the Antichrist. We now have our two tests: does a sign or wonder lead me to worship God or something else? Does the spirit or entity confess Jesus as coming in the flesh?

Chapter 29

Aliens and Extra Terrestrial Life

If the definition of "alien" is strictly, "a being who was not born on earth," technically all angels, demons, and even God Himself can be considered aliens. However, the popular use of the term is referring to life on other planets apart from any of the spiritual entities in the Bible. Aliens to the people that believe in them are either "flesh and blood," as in they are like humans just a different species and from another place, or entities that exist in a higher plane of existence. We will examine flesh and blood extra terrestrials first.

The theory of life on other planets has been around for a long time, but the current form was largely influenced by Erich von Daniken and his 1968 book *Chariots of the Gods*. While the theory of extra terrestrial life interacting with earth life remained a fringe theory in the sense that not many people believed or talked about it, the idea has gained a lot of traction in the last decade or so. Proponents such as Giogio Tsoukalos, Dr. Steven Greer, and organizations such as MUFON (Mutual UFO Network) have spread the theory very effectively throughout the culture. The *Ancient Aliens* documentary series aired on the

History Channel was also a big factor in spreading this theory.

There are two main areas proponents focus on when talking about their theories: aliens in the past and aliens in the present. Proponents who focus on aliens in the past, sometimes called Ancient Astronaut theorists, look at megalithic structures built by ancient civilizations and deduce they couldn't be built by only humans and their known tools. They also use religious texts—such as the Bible or the Hindu Vedas—by reinterpreting them using aliens and their supposed technology in place of gods, angels, or whatever spiritual beings are in the text. Furthermore, they look at science and biology and admit life couldn't have started by evolution (I agree with them!). But instead of looking to a supernatural Creator, they say aliens with gene manipulation technology modified earth life into humans. There are many other "evidences" the ancient astronaut theory uses to support their views, but the above examples are some of the most popular.

The other main area of the theory of alien existence is alien encounters in the present. Proponents focusing on this area research UFO encounters, abductions, and any other phenomena they consider "alien contact." They try to answer questions such as "Why are the aliens here?" or "What message are they communicating to us?" Another big topic in this community is researching government cover ups or disclosures that "prove" governments are hiding an alien presence from the world's population. Many times researchers of "alien encounters" become aware of massive government corruption and even the ways the world is being pushed toward a one world government, but they do not make the connection that Satan is the one directing these events.

Whether looking at the past or the present, whenever a person has an encounter with so-called aliens, we do not necessarily doubt their experience, although there is chance they imagined or made it up. It is better to understand how to interpret an experience rather than deny it.

In the case of aliens, there are many things about human history that are strange and make us wonder how humans achieved the feats they accomplished. In the modern day, I believe people do see lights in the sky or whatever else they encounter. I also believe encounters are "aliens" in the sense of beings not from this earth. But if we run the idea of aliens and alien encounters through our tests of Scripture, we find demons are actually the "aliens."

Does the sign or wonder of aliens lead us to worship God or something else? Of all the documentaries and books about aliens I have watched or read, never has anyone worshiped God because of historical research about aliens or an alien encounter. Instead, people who research or seek encounters often get involved in transcendental meditation, worshiping the earth, or are so focused on alien research they never consider God in their life. Deuteronomy 4:19 even warns us not to worship the stars, which is where aliens are said to come from. Proponents of the theory of alien life often push agendas such as world peace, environmentalism, or free energy for everyone. These things in themselves are not bad; for example, I would like to see the world in peace or people take better care of the planet. However, these things will not be made right until Jesus returns.

Before He returns, there will be another false christ that comes and will most likely claim to have a solution to the problems alien theorists point out. If the alien theory is not leading to Christ as humanity's Savior, it is leading to the Antichrist instead. Ultimately, alien theorists do not encourage people to believe in or follow God. Their theories and agendas push people away from worshiping Him and His truth.

Before moving onto our other test of a sign or wonder, not only could alien abductions be an explanation for the Rapture, but they could be used as a way to deter people from faith in Jesus during the Tribulation. There will be many signs in the sky from God in the seal, bowl, and trumpet judgments. Satan may say different alien races are performing the signs to deceive people from thinking these judgments are from God. Also, as demons eventually do not conceal themselves (Revelation 16:14), they may pose as the "good" race of aliens fighting against the "bad" race of aliens, the bad race being God and His angels.

Do these spirits, or "aliens," confess Jesus as coming in the flesh? "Aliens" do apparently communicate with humans, as there are many who claim they have communicated with aliens. If we don't doubt the experience but rather the interpretation of it, these "aliens" are actually demons talking with people. I am not aware of any communication from aliens confessing Jesus as God and Savior of the world. Anyone that has talked about their communication with aliens has never mentioned Jesus at all. It would be interesting to ask alien visitors what they think of Jesus of Nazareth. I think it would be very obvious they do not confess Him as Savior.

Since the sign of aliens do not direct us to God or confess Jesus as coming in the flesh, this must be a demonic sign. It is true we do not see demons in the Bible appearing as orbs of light in the sky or in the shape of a flying craft. While we are never given a shape for Satan or demons, angels do appear with light (Matthew 28:3, Luke 24:4). Since "Satan himself transforms himself into an angel of light" (II Corinthians 11:14), he and his demons may use the appearance of light to deceive people.

Alien abductions are hard to explain, yet Satan and demons' power seem to fit with descriptions of this type of encounter. Satan is able to show visions (Luke 4:5) and transport a person to different locations very quickly (Luke 4:9). If demons have this power too, it would explain the visions and location differences

Aliens and Extra Terrestrial Life

of people's experiences. As for the physical probing abductions, Satan was given power over Job's body (Job 2:6-7) and demons can cause various bodily effects and physical deformations (Mark 9:17-27, Luke 13:11). Satan was even given permission to kill Job's servants (Job 1:16). If Satan and demons can have this kind of power over a human's body and give them visions, it is not a stretch for me to believe they could show a person a vision of a space ship and also handle their physical body.

UFO sightings may also be a combination of demon appearances and human technology. It is very possible groups of humans have technology of which we are not aware; it is not farfetched to think there are non-government groups able to develop and build objects we might interpret as alien craft. These groups may even expose these inventions to government scientists, call it an alien spaceship, and then have those very smart people research it and come up with new technology. Could demons assist in building or help with the function of technology? There is no record of this in the Bible, but given their ability to manipulate matter, it is certainly possible.

One other important point about alien sightings is that they seem to change over time. Back in the 1940's and 50's, sightings largely included what looked like some kind of craft. Today, encounters include more orbs of light rather than vehicles. While this observation is a bit anecdotal, if aliens really were just a different type of life form, one would expect consistency in their form. Alien theorists explain this by talking about the many species of aliens that inhabit the galaxy. However, looking through a Biblical lens, the demons are reacting to different societal norms to be as deceptive as possible. Demons are quite smart and we should not be surprised if they change their behavior or appearance to deceive cultures.

As with many of the topics we will be discussing in this section, I do not have all the answers and explanations such as how every alien encounter is actually a demon encounter. What I do know is aliens do not point people to God, which means we should not be involved in trying to contact or encounter them. If we have had a past encounter or encounter them in the future, we have not necessarily done anything wrong, but we should be able to interpret this experience in light of God's Word.

Chapter 30

Cryptozoology

Cryptozoology is the study of animals not yet recognized by "main stream science." While there are almost certainly many species of animals we have not discovered, this chapter is devoted to the "mystical" creatures of Cryptozoology, such as Bigfoot/Sasquatch, the Yeti, Mothman, skinwalkers, or any other such animal that has some sort of spiritual connection. I will focus mostly on Bigfoot because that is the "animal" with which most people are familiar.

Bigfoot is claimed by some to be an ape-like animal that is not spiritual at all; they believe he is an animal like any other animal we know, but cannot prove his existence without a doubt. Others believe he is an alien; they reason he can travel through different dimensions or phase in and out of our visible world which explains how he evades detection. The American Indians believed Bigfoot was a spiritual creature and revered him as such. The people of Tibet also look at the Yeti in a similar way.

One piece of evidence which is very common in Bigfoot sightings is the element of fear in the person who encounters him. People often talk about the terror they experience from seeing or even just hearing what they interpret as Bigfoot. There are no other creatures on earth that illicit this emotional response in such a wide range of encounters. This evidence is what makes me believe Bigfoot is not just an animal, but something else. The only other option is a sign or wonder from a demon.

Does Bigfoot or any other mystical-type creature lead people to worship God? In the same way as aliens, I have never heard any cryptozoolgist talk about faith in God because of their research into these creatures. I do not hear cryptozoologists push any agendas like the alien theorists very often, probably because they are focused on proving their theory rather than other ideas. If these creatures are sourced in demonic power, they are more likely a distraction from God rather than a direct deception into believing something other than God. Some demons are less evil than others (Luke 11:24-26), so maybe the less evil demons are involved in this distraction while the more evil demons are involved in other signs and wonders. These creatures could also be regular animals, but I believe the sum of all the evidence speaks otherwise.

Do any mystical animals confess Jesus in the flesh? I'm not aware of any credible stories of these animals communicating with humans through language, so this test is not necessarily applicable to this topic.

While it is certainly interesting to look for undiscovered animals, we should be careful about time devoted to the practice as well as realizing when there is a spiritual element involved in the creature.

Chapter 31

Magic in Entertainment

Spiritual themes are very common in our modern world of movies, video games, music, shows on television or the internet, board games, and anything else with which we entertain ourselves. Magic and spiritual beings are often plot devices or mechanisms of how characters do things. Demons are not necessarily used on the set of movies, although it is possible. In other forms of entertainment, there are many accounts of a "spiritual presence" during music concerts or software developers who are working on horror-type video games having grotesque nightmares. New ways to contact demons are wrapped with an entertainment veneer, such as Ouija boards or even apps on our phones and computers that teach us how to contact spiritual entities.

How we entertain ourselves or what we do to relax is a personal decision between each person in God. We have liberty in Christ and if I were to give commands, such as, "thou shalt not watch such-and-such movies," this would be legalism and only give the appearance of wisdom in self-imposed religion (Colossians 2:20-23). However, to say the things we watch, music we listen to, or games we play do not influence us would be far from the truth.

In Deuteronomy 13, the same chapter from which we get one of our key tests for signs and wonders, God gives instruction to the children of Israel that when a city goes and serves other gods, they should gather all the things from that city and burn them (Deuteronomy 13:12-18). In fact, God even calls the plunder from the city "accursed things" in verse 17. As we have said before, the Church is not under the Mosiac law, and we are not commanded to burn things as the Israelites were. But we can learn a principle from this passage: God cares about the physical items in our homes and how they effect our relationship with Him.

While the ancient cultures surrounding the Israelites did not have videos, images we see in a digital format also impact our walk with God. Even though the people on a screen may be acting, the things their characters are doing are still subject to God's Word and we should look at them through the lens of Scripture. For example, if a movie portrays an intimate scene between two people in a bedroom, they may be "acting" out the sexual act (although this is not always the case), but we are still viewing their real uncovered bodies and actions. In the same way, if a movie portrays magical powers, I am consuming these spiritual themes and they can impact my life.

To be clear, I am not saying everyone who watches a movie with magic will become a witch, nor am I condemning every video with a spiritual theme. I am simply saying entertainment impacts our walk with God, and we should test the spiritual themes in entertainment by Scripture for whether we should participate in it or not.

Another principle relevant to the topic of spiritual themes in entertainment is caring about our brothers and sisters in Christ. Even though we may think a certain show or video is fine to

Magic in Entertainment

watch, another believer around us may not hold the same conviction. If your brother or sister is grieved, "you are no longer walking in love" (Romans 14:15). If our freedom to entertain ourselves grieves someone we are around, we should stop doing it in their presence.

We should not be legalistic about our choices, but we should be very careful about the objects, whether physical or digital, we allow in our homes and how they may effect ourselves and others. Are they leading me to worship God or not? Are the things I invest my time in for entertainment bringing me closer to Him or at least not drawing me away? It is a personal question for each person to answer, and while we should take this idea seriously, we should not be judgmental of others if we do not agree with their choices (Romans 14:10-13). "Therefore let us pursue the things which make for peace and the things by which one may edify another" (Romans 14:19).

Chapter 32

Modern Rituals of Divination and Magic

How to perform divination and magic has evolved since the Bible was written. This is one way Romans 1:30 is fulfilled, which says unbelievers will be "inventors of evil things." Séances, palmistry, fortune-telling, horoscopes, spells, potions, and any other ritual may not be new, but new ways of doing them is always appearing. For example, computers may be used to create horoscopes. New potions may be concocted with ingredients unavailable to witches in the past. New spells may be cast as the world has gotten bigger and there are different motivations.

Rituals and magic are also strange things to research because there are many different views and ways to practice it. Some witches, male or female, believe in many different planes of existence and altering those planes to change reality. Other witches try to contact spirits directly to perform their spells. Witches can be religious by worshiping various deities while other witches don't believe in any spiritual beings. In fact, sometimes the definition of "magic" cannot be agreed on. I believe the truest Biblical definition of magic is contacting spiritual entities other than God to manipulate creation, but witches may not agree with this.

One thing for certain is divination and magic are more accepted than they were in times past. I have watched documentaries in which the host participates in a ritual of witchcraft or demonic possession. And as the world becomes more connected, we will continue to see a blending of practices from across the world; for example, European witches may incorporate into their rituals Hindu meditation practices which were previously unknown.

Secret teachings are also becoming more talked about. For example, the practices and beliefs of Freemasonry used to be guarded secrets by Freemasons, but now more people are talking about the occult beliefs and rituals which are part of higher levels of the organization. The Kabbalah, the book and practice of Jewish mysticism, is also more readily mentioned in connection with groups and people who follow it's teaching. From the beginning, Satan enticed humans with "secret knowledge" they would only gain if they do what he says (Genesis 3:5). Any "secret knowledge" is doctrine Satan gives humans to get them to believe in things other than God for salvation. No matter how fantastical this knowledge may seem, the power he offers us, or how Satan may confirm his doctrine with signs and wonders, everything we need to know and do is contained in the Bible: "All Scripture is given by inspiration of God, and is profitable for doctrine, for reproof, for correction, for instruction in righteousness, that the man of God may be complete, thoroughly equipped for every good work" (II Timothy 3:16-17). The Bible tells us what to believe (doctrine), what not to believe (reproof), what not to do (correction), and what to do (instruction in righteousness).

I included this chapter not to give an exhaustive list of all modern divination and magic practices, for that would be

Modern Rituals of Divination and Magic

impossible. Furthermore, I have not participated in magic or divination so there is much I do not know without first hand experience. But these practices are certainly real and do work to some degree, and it is pertinent to explain new ideas within these arts for us to recognize them when we see them. Although there are other good ways to use discernment, our two tests are an excellent place to start; is this ritual bringing me to worship God and do contacted spirits confess Jesus in the flesh?

Chapter 33

Transhumanism

Transhumanism is the belief that humans can use technology to enhance or transform humans beyond how God created us. This belief system is becoming popular among the global elites as technology continues to advance. Transhumanists believe humans can integrate with a digital world, even forfeiting our human bodies and becoming data. *Pharmekeia* may be used during the end times as one of the ideas to transform humanity by injected ourselves with drugs that manipulate our DNA.

Transhumanists are starting to become open about their ultimate goals, which is to either build themselves their own god through technology or become "gods" themselves by transcending their humanity. One transhumanist goal, at least for the masses not necessarily the elites, is to create an entire digital world humans are able to "plug into" and leave their physical bodies behind. This is not just a rejection of the body with which God created us; it is a rejection of God's entire creation.

Transhumanists that believe in creating their own digital world are seeking to give themselves eternal life apart from faith in Jesus Christ by integrating their soul with technology. In this way, they become their own saviors and creators. Not all transhumanists are aiming for the same goals, so just like magic or witchcraft, the definition of transhumanism is different depending on the transhumanist with whom you are talking.

Does using technology to transcend my humanity bring me to worship God? I don't think it is possible, since the very foundation of transhumanism is our human bodies are either insufficient or need to evolve. God created us as a soul connected to a body (Genesis 2:7), and when we get to heaven He will give us a new body (I Corinthians 15:35-49). Nowhere in the Bible does it indicate we need anything other than the body and reality God created for us. God gives us instruction for how to live in both His current creation and the world to come. We should not seek to alter His gifts to us by fundamentally changing His creation or trying to build our own.

Transhumaists don't necessarily contact demons, although there are some who believe aliens can help us transcend our bodies and world. As we studied before, aliens are demons masquerading as beings from other planets and will not confess Jesus as coming in the flesh. I do not know of any popular transhumanists who confess Jesus as Savior either. If any transhumanists are involved in contacting demons in their quest for the singularity (becoming one with technology), it cannot lead to a proclamation of the Gospel and Jesus as the Savior of humanity.

Chapter 34

Meditation, Visions, and Remote Viewing

Meditation is the practice of focusing on a single idea or emptying the mind to ascend to a higher plane of consciousness. Meditation as focusing on a single thought is not bad; in fact, prayer could be considered a form of meditation because we're focused on God and communicating with Him. But when meditation is focused on "not thinking" or "emptying your mind," this is not a Biblical concept. God tells us to renew our mind "that you may prove what is that good and acceptable and perfect will of God" (Romans 12:2). In Isaiah 1:18 God says, "Come now, and let us reason together" which is using our minds rather than emptying them.

Why are we talking about meditation in a book about Satan and demons' power? In a form of meditation called TM or transcendental meditation, those who meditate tell stories of having thoughts put in their head, hearing voices, or actually talking to beings in their mind. This type of meditation is closely linked to remote viewing or astral projection, a very old practice. Remote viewing is the ability to travel outside your body and go anywhere in the universe or another dimension.

Visions do not necessarily have to happen during meditation. There are many stories of people being transported to different locations from the past, having nature change around them, people appearing and communicating with them, or visions during dreams. The visions may even be partly authentic in terms of traveling to different locations, for Satan is able to transport humans around the globe (Luke 4:9). These experiences often have a great impact on the person experiencing the vision, sometimes changing the entire course of their life.

As with other strange encounters, we don't necessarily discredit the experience; but the interpretation of the experience must stand the test of Scripture. I have never had an "out of body" experience or immersive vision, nor have I ever meditated to a point of talking with otherworldly beings or hearing voices. Because of this, there is a level of ignorance on my part to interpret what is going on. Using Scripture, my best guess is demons have the same power as Satan to transport humans quickly to different locations and make visions appear (Luke 4:5, 9). When someone meditates on something other than God, this seems to be opening oneself to demonic communication. When someone astral projects themselves, this may be demons showing them visions during their meditation. God breathed life into our body (Genesis 2:7), so it does not seem possible to leave our body at our will.

Does remote viewing or meditation lead me to worship God? I have never heard someone using these practices support correct Biblical theology. There are believers who participate in practices of this form, but the messages they receive and the experiences they have do not align with what the Bible says about spiritual experiences. We are never told to try to travel outside our body or seek entities in our meditative times. We are to focus on God and His truth during times of prayer instead of astral projection or transcendental meditation.

Meditation, Visions, and Remote Viewing

Do entities contacted during meditation confess Jesus in the flesh? I have never heard anyone talk about entities confessing this. Any beings contacted through these rituals, which can only be demons, often tell people the same things aliens tell people, which should tell us the same entities are involved in both signs. Instead of using practices like meditation or remote viewing, we should use the practices God gives us in His Word to draw closer to Him, such as prayer, reading the Scriptures, singing songs, and gathering together as believers.

Chapter 35

Chi/Qi/Ki and Vital Energy

The idea of chi (there are multiple spellings including qi and ki) comes from Asian countries surrounding China. Chi is "vital energy," or an energy that flows throughout the body and must be kept in balance for good health. Chi, they say, is also found in all things in the universe and links them together. It is a fundamental concept for Chinese medicine and is used for combat in Asian martial arts.

Having done martial arts and learned combat and healing applications rooted in Chinese medicine, there is truth to how they look at the body and health. When a marital artist applies chi concepts to their techniques, the results are stronger and more effective. There is no ritual to call upon spirits for help or any spiritual forces at work; the technique is applying ways God has already built our bodies to either cause pain or heal. What exactly is happening when using chi in combat has been studied but is hard to explain, although it is often related to the electricity that runs through our bodies.

However, contention comes with the Bible when fully applying the belief system surrounding chi. Chi as the vital

Deceiving by Signs

energy or force of the universe is strongly influenced by Buddhism and other Chinese spiritual beliefs. Qigong is the practice of building up one's chi and this practice shares similarities with transcendental meditation. There are many schools of thought on qigong, but most carry common themes such as emptying your mind or feeling energy from all things running through your body. This can open a person to demonic contact in the same way as transcendental meditation.

Yet it is important to remember Chinese medicine was developed in a cultural context just like Western medicine. As the Chinese were discovering ways to treat ailments or make a self defense technique stronger, their religion and culture influenced the explanation for why something worked. Western medicine is similar if you consider medical practice in the last one hundred years was largely influence by Rockefeller and an interest in selling drugs that are petroleum based. Medicine in the west has not been attached to a "religion," but that is not to say the culture and people who funded medical study did not influence the "whys" of a certain treatment working.

The reason I'm contrasting the Chinese and Western medical systems is to make us aware that just because Chinese medicine attaches religious thought to their practice does not make it untrue or demonic. There are many ideas or applications of chi that look very strange or even demonic to a western mind, yet there is no ritual contacting demons or any demonic influence on what is being done. It is possible for a nonbeliever to use chi and also have a demon influence events, making a situation difficult to interpret just like other signs in this section. But even though chi and Chinese medicine are foreign concepts and not necessarily demonic, the ideas are interwoven into pagan ideas which can open the practitioner to demonic influence.

Does chi lead me to worship God? This question can be hard to answer; when I learn about ways to defend myself or heal using the concept of chi and Chinese medicine, I do worship God for the intricate way He created our bodies even though I may not fully understand the reason something works. But if I look at the belief system of chi, those ideas can lead me away from worshiping Him. God created the universe and our bodies in amazingly intricate ways, but just as our bodies can be used for good and evil, we should be careful about pagan belief systems.

Chapter 36

Psychics

Psychics in the modern day are ultimately diviners, sorcerers, mediums or a combination of practitioners connected with demonic power. Psychics can offer a range of services such as contacting dead relatives, helping police solve cases, or water dousing. We have already studied all the arts psychics are involved in, but I wanted to bring them up because they appear on our TVs and computer screens and are used in a variety of ways. They are certainly tapping into demonic power to get information. If the information is about the past, we should not be surprised if demons give them correct information because the demons could have been around when an event occurred. The Bible recognizes demons' predictions about the future will come true occasionally (Deuteronomy 13:2), but they are only making an educated guess from their knowledge and ability to influence events.

Will being a psychic or going to a psychic for information lead me to worship God? I cannot think of a way going to someone who will give me guesses at best and information from demons at worst will make me worship God. The fact I am seeking information or help from something other than God is not honoring to Him at all. We should have nothing to do with psychics and their practices except to give them the Gospel if there is an opportunity.

Do spirits contacted by psychics confess Jesus in the flesh? I have never heard of this happening but quite the opposite. If Jesus is brought up to an entity summoned by a psychic, there can be violent and angry reactions by the spirit. They do not like Jesus, and a psychic will never encourage people to place their faith in Christ but rather faith in their practices.

Chapter 37

Modern Demon Possession

Modern stories of demon possession gets a small chapter because there were questions that may have popped up after the chapter on what the Bible says about demon possession. I have not been involved in any exorcisms, so like some other topics in this section, there is a level of ignorance on my part to confess.

I have heard descriptions of demon possessed people that can speak with different voices and languages, levitate, vomit an enormous amount of fluid not possible to be contained in one body, act fine when the demons have not left, blackened eyes, and many other descriptions. The Bible does not give us a lot of detail of what happens during an exorcism nor other possible qualities and abilities a demon possessed person may have. The Bible seems to allow for most modern descriptions of demon possession to be true, but we should make sure we are grounded in the Scriptures instead of focusing on the sometimes fantastical stories of possession.

There are also manuals of techniques for how to exorcise demons using holy water, crucifixes, or other such rituals and

Deceiving by Signs

objects. While demons may react to these things, unclean spirits are also masters of deception. During a exorcism, they could certainly react deceptively to exorcism practices to increase falsehood of how possession actually works or how to effectively get them out of someone's body. The Biblical pattern of exorcism is using Jesus' Name through words to immediately make the demon leave except for the mention of some exorcisms needing prayer and fasting (Mark 9:29). If we are ever in a situation of demon possession, keeping to what Scripture says and relying on Jesus' power will not lead us astray.

Chapter 38

Satanic Worship

Satan worship is sometimes laughed at and assumed to not be something people do. But there are definitely people worshiping Satan, whether it was Anton LaVey who wrote the Satanic Bible or another Satanic cult. The rituals performed in Satan worship often mirror Christian rituals but pervert them. In some denominations of Satanism, religious ceremonies will have communion, but they do not do it in remembrance of Jesus' death; rather they change the elements of communion, such as substituting real blood and flesh from human sacrifice instead of wine/juice and bread. Rituals are not only for the purpose of worshiping Satan, but also for gaining spiritual power over other people. Satan worshipers often believe Satan will grant them power for their allegiance and make them successful in their life. There are also many stories across the world of people being brutally abused during Satanic rituals. These stories are often very violent, and I will repeat none of the horrific details in this book.

However, not all Satan worship is directed toward Lucifer. Some that would call themselves "Satanists" do not acknowledge Lucifer as a being, but rather a collective evil in the world or within each person. Satanism, just like Christianity or any other religious system, has denominations following different sets of beliefs. However, in whatever form it takes, Satanism ultimately affirms selfish and prideful desires of sinful man.

I do not encourage anyone to research the topic of Satan worship unless they are led by God to do so, for it is very dark and you must be spiritually mature to handle the information. There are many rituals of worship and groups involved; by design, the hierarchy and practices are shrouded in mystery, so it can be difficult to know the truth about what goes on during rituals or what certain practices actually are and why they are done. However, Scripture tells us one day the world will worship the Antichrist and Lucifer (Revelation 13:4), so we should be prepared for Satan worship becoming more prevalent in our day.

Chapter 39

Disease and Mental Illness

We know Satan and demons can cause disease and mental instability (Job 2:7, Mark 9:17-18), and there is no reason to think they have stopped doing these things in our time. While there is not much to say on this topic other than we should be aware some diseases can be caused by demons, there are many stories of mental health facilities having teams of believers who perform "special treatments" for patients. The special treatments can be exorcisms or sessions of prayer for those with mental conditions. I do not know the exact practices they use for these treatments, but there certainly are cases in which people sent to these facilities are not sick with natural diseases but have demons impacting their health. Both the patients and believers helping them need prayer.

Chapter 40

Natural Disasters

Whenever there is a large natural disaster or a number of disasters in quick succession, there will inevitably be a mention of Matthew 24:7-8. The relevant part of this passage to natural disasters says, "There will be... earthquakes in various places. All these are the beginning of sorrows." While this passage is dealing with the Tribulation not our current age, Satan is capable of manipulating nature's forces, such as a great wind (Job 1:19). When natural disasters occur, there is a chance they are not "natural," but are caused by Satan to further his goal of being like God (Isaiah 1:13-14). While I think these times are rare, Satan very frequently uses the chaos of disasters, whether natural or planned, to move the world closer to a one world government. We should be aware of his power over nature, yet not immediately assume he is the cause of something that happens.

It also could be true that natural disasters could become more frequent as we move closer to the Tribulation just as we see the world being prepared in other ways. However, there is no direct Biblical evidence for this, so we should be cautious to

Deceiving by Signs

interpret disasters as a signs the Tribulation is imminent.

Chapter 41
Sexual Desires and Sex with Demons

From our previous studies, we know demons can have sex (Genesis 6:4) and Satan will sexually tempt married couples when they are apart and lack self control (I Corinthians 7:5). Satan and demons are not afraid to get involved in sexual interactions. The Bible often mentions our sexual desires as causing us to sin and tells us very pointedly to "Flee sexual immorality" (I Corinthians 6:18). Satan knows how easily ensnared by our lust we are, and people also know how much money can be made by marketing to our sexual desires. Aside from the temptation to give into lust, this short chapter deals with the spiritual side of demonic sexuality.

There are claims and books written about having sex with spiritual entities. Some even claim to be married to spiritual beings and write about their experiences of being married to a non-human. Some denominations of Satanism even have rituals of "sex magic," in which magical power is sought or attempts made to conceive a child with some sort of special power. There are even stories of women being visited during the night and a demon enticing them into sexual acts.

Deceiving by Signs

While I realize I have not cited any of these claims to bring them more authenticity, I can assure you these stories and experiences are real to the people who have them. The Bible certainly allows for demons to be able to participate or be involved in sexual acts with humans. Revelation makes it very clear one of the main characteristics of the Babylon of the end times will be fornication (Revelation 17:2-5, 18:3). Perhaps sex will be used as a comfort for unbelievers during the Tribulation who are experiencing the woes of the trumpet, seal, and bowl judgments. Babylon will "become a dwelling place of demons," (Revelation 18:2) and it is possible these demons will be involved in the fornication so prevalent in the city. While we do not see sex with spiritual entities being mentioned as much as aliens or Cryptozoology in our culture, eventually stories of sex with non-humans could become more mainstream.

Chapter 42

Influence on Government

When studying demons, the angel who visited Daniel to explain his vision said, "The prince of the kingdom of Persia withstood me twenty-one days; and behold, Michael, one of the chief princes, came to help me... And now I must return to fight with the prince of Persia" (Daniel 10:13, 20). We explained a human prince could not stop angels from traveling, so there must be demons "behind the throne" of earthly kingdoms, fighting spiritual battles on behalf of humans against God's servants. Satan also has authority over all the kingdoms of the world (Luke 4:6).

This means Satan and demons have influence over government and politicians. There could be a speech, a law, a court ruling, an executive order, or even a department created through the influence of demons. Politicians, judges, and any other government worker is not necessarily possessed, but we should be aware of the effect demons can have in governmental affairs.

While I don't think Paul is strictly talking about government, it is true in terms of our fight for freedom from oppressive

Deceiving by Signs

government is not "against flesh and blood, but against principalities, against powers, against the rulers of the darkness of this age, against spiritual hosts of wickedness in the heavenly places" (Ephesians 6:12). We should be praying for all our government officials, for protection against demonic forces and to be saved if they are not already.

As we grow closer to the Rapture, we need to realize God has already ordained the world, especially it's governments, to be more wicked in the latter times (I Timothy 4:1, II Timothy 3:1-13); yet we are still to offer supplications, prayers, intercessions, and giving of thanks "for all men, for kings and all who are in authority, that we may lead a quiet and peaceable life in all godliness and reverence" (I Timothy 2:1-2). The quieter and more peaceable our lives as believers are, even in the midst of government oppression, the more we can share the Gospel, for God "desires all men to be saved and to come to the knowledge of the truth" (I Timothy 2:4).

Chapter 43

Evil Places and Sites

The end times Babylon will eventually "become a dwelling place of demons" (Revelation 18:2). Demons seem to congregate where there is a lot of evil, and this Biblical evidence allows for places on earth in which an uneasy feeling falls upon those who travel to those locations. There are places I have been and heard stories where there is a bad atmosphere amidst the place. There could be a feeling of someone watching you, a sick feeling in the stomach, or even a feeling you shouldn't be there and to get out immediately.

These feelings could be the Holy Spirit warning of demons or the demons letting their presence be known to those who go there; it also could be the innate sense of fear God put in our consciousness to protect ourselves. While demons could certainly be present at these places, it is also possible we could be working ourselves into being afraid when there is nothing to be afraid of.

Many TV shows film at or go to "haunted" or paranormal locations to entertain or document supernatural activity at the site. While there are certainly faked reactions and events having a perfectly normal explanation, people have experiences during these expeditions that are absolutely demonic in nature. There is often just enough truth mixed in with acting to keep the identity of the paranormal entities shrouded to those who do not view these events through a Biblical lens.

There are also many stories of apparitions appearing at these sites or even in very normal places. These encounters are the source of many ghost stories and commonly have a dead person reappearing as a spirit or some sort of shape materializing that is human-like. Angels and other heavenly creatures are described as fiery (II Kings 6:17), having wings (Isaiah 6:2), full of eyes (Revelation 4:6), having animal faces or multiple faces (Revelation 4:7, Ezekiel 1:10), or just a generally magnificent appearance (Daniel 10:5-6). Since we are never given a description of a demon's appearance other than the locusts of Revelation 9:3-10, we don't know the form(s) they can take. If angels can have a glorious appearance, can demons appear with an appearance just as striking but in a grotesque way? It is definitely possible, and if so it would explain apparitions and many other ghostly forms people have encountered throughout the world and over the centuries.

If any place ever gives a person a feeling they should not be there, they see something they can't explain, or they feel there is just something off, the best thing to do is trust the feeling and leave immediately. We should also not intentionally go to places where there may be demonic activity, such as participating in "ghost hunts," visiting "haunted" locations, or anything like that. If demons are present, they can use their abilities to draw people away from God and to seek alternate sources of beliefs about the supernatural.

DECEPTION OF GOD'S TRIBULATION JUDGMENTS

The Tribulation will include many signs and wonders, most notably the trumpet, seal, and bowl judgments. Satan will also be doing signs for the purpose of deceiving mankind into worshiping him. But he will not only deceive people through supernatural power but also doctrine, false reasoning, and logic. If we look at just the trumpet, seal, and bowl judgments, what are ways Satan could explain away God's signs to deceive people into not turning to Him in faith? This section, like the last, is speculation, but it is a good exercise to think about how Satan could reason those signs away or justify people to perform acts they would never think to do or support without his influence. Many of the same deceptive ideas in our day may be used in the Tribulation as well.

A running theme through each sign from God may be Satan calling God and his angels an alien race which is coming to destroy humanity. The Antichrist may also call Satan and his demons a good alien race coming to save mankind from the "bad" aliens. I mention this because this could be a deception for almost every seal, trumpet, or bowl. As we discussed in the alien

Deceiving by Signs

chapter, this is becoming a more accepted theory and Satan may be preparing the world for his deception of the identity of God.

How much unbelievers realize about God, His power, and why He is bringing His wrath on the earth during the Tribulation is unknown, however they do recognize Him and Jesus as the source of the signs (Revelation 6:16). One would think if they understood fully without deception, they would all believe in Jesus, but this will not happen. Satan's deception is so strong that people will have at least a basic understanding of God, yet still worship the Antichrist and Satan instead (II Thessalonians 2:11-12).

Chapter 44

Deception of the Seals

The first seal is the revealing of the Antichrist (Revelation 6:1-2). He is described as being on a white horse just as Jesus comes on a white horse (Revelation 19:11). The Antichrist will be presented to the world as a savior, offering solutions to all the world's problems. The world will not realize he will not be the savior they think he is but instead will cause more problems and death than any other earthly ruler ever has.

Leaders being likened to Jesus or called a messiah is being done in our day. One of the most recent examples is President Barack Obama who was called a messiah and compared to Jesus during his presidential campaign. I encourage you to do research on the number of politicians that have been called saviors, messiahs, or been given religious significance in order to gain popularity with the people. This tactic is not new, and it is certainly one way the Antichrist could be presented to the world.

The second seal is taking peace from the earth and having people kill each other (Revelation 6:3-4). People will be given reasons to fight each other and surely many people will die. In our day, we see many ways Satan uses differences in people to divide us, such as race, sexual orientation, views on health, etc. These divisions will become so strong people will kill each other over them; however, each side will mostly likely view themselves as the "good guys" under divine authority to rid the earth of the terribleness of the "bad guys." Dividing people and influencing them to hate another group of people is common in our day and will probably be used in the Tribulation.

When the third seal is opened, there will be a lack of food on the earth (Revelation 6:5-6). This shortage sounds like it is due to inflation of prices and shortages. Even today, prices are constantly going up; during the early 2020's inflation increased at alarming rates. The media always gives the public reasons for why inflation and shortages happen, but these are not always the real or complete reason. The supply for a certain item could be very low, but often it is corporations raising prices arbitrarily to make more money or to create an artificial panic to then offer a solution which increases their control of the world's food supply. The same patterns we see today seem to appear in the Tribulation as well, and I encourage you to research how the food and money supply is controlled by the banks and corporations.

The next seal will kill a fourth of the earth, with the sword, hunger, death and beasts of the earth (Revelation 6:7-8). The inflation and food shortages of the third seal will most likely be the catalyst to this seal; an easy decision to make when there is a famine is to remove the number of people that need food. One common lie being told by Satan today is the world's population is too large. This is not true, but we are told we are killing the earth through the number of people, and we will either run out of resources or the earth can't sustain itself. Eugenics, although its never called that anymore, is suggested as the solution to the "problem" as well as save-the-planet efforts.

In the Tribulation, there is a good chance these same ideas will be used to justify the killing of one fourth of the earth's population. If there is a shortage of food and Satan has successfully divided the earth into groups of people willing to kill each other after the second seal, killing the "undesirables" of the world will be an easy decision to make for those who consider themselves better than others and want to "save the earth." I do not know how the beasts of the earth get involved; maybe animals are also so hungry they attack people? Maybe there are animals used in the armies that will execute people? Demons are able to enter animals (Mark 5:13) and maybe demons possess the animals to kill people as part of the fourth seal.

The fifth seal is the cry of martyrs killed during the Tribulation (Revelation 6:9-11). During the previous four seals and after, many believers who preach the Gospel of the kingdom will be killed. Martyrdom will reach its height during the Tribulation. Believers and Jews will most likely be blamed for the world's problems like they are today in various ways. After what we've seen as possibilities to explain away the first four seals, believers being killed will not be a problem for many people to go along with. The two witnesses will also be around during this time causing havoc by their power for those who want to harm them (Revelation 11:5-6). There will be a great harvest of souls during the Tribulation but also many martyrs. Throughout this time Satan will be getting the world to go along with mass holocausts as much as possible.

In the sixth seal there is a great earthquake and many strange things happening in the sky (Revelation 6:12-17). It is so bad with things falling to earth that the world's population hides themselves in caves and mountains They apparently know God is doing it because they say "Fall on us and hide us from the face of Him who sits on the throne and from the wrath of the Lamb!

Deceiving by Signs

For the great day of His wrath has come, and who is able to stand?" (Revelation 12:16-17).

One would think this sort of sign in which the people know God is the source would cause them to turn from following the Antichrist and to believe in Jesus instead. However, that won't happen (Revelation 9:21). With what will Satan deceive them? I am unsure on this seal because the world knows God is executing His judgment. One example of people being stubborn and not turning from sin when God's signs are so obvious is the Israelites and their exodus from Egypt. God displayed His power in magnificent ways, however they still did not trust Him all the time, such as doubting they could defeat the Canaanites (Numbers 13-14). Just as the children of Israel did not trust God back then even though they had every piece of evidence to do so, many people during the Tribulation will react the same way.

The seventh seal includes the trumpet and bowl judgments, so we will discuss each of those in their own chapter.

Chapter 45

Deception of the Trumpets

The first trumpet is trees and grass burned up by hail and fire mingled with blood (Revelation 8:7). Satan may imitate this sign through the false prophet who can also make fire come down from heaven (Revelation 13:13). By this time, mankind may have found alternate food sources from vegetation, so they may not regard trees and grass getting burned up as important. Pride may also be involved by the Antichrist telling mankind he is so great they don't need plants for food anymore because he has provided other ways of sustenance.

The next trumpet has something like a great mountain burning with fire hitting the sea making a third of the sea blood as well as destroying a third of both sea creatures and ships (Revelation 8:8-9). We know demons can make water blood (Exodus 7:22) so this would be another case where God's sign could be mimicked and reasoned away. The blood could also be from the massive amounts of sea creatures and sailors dying. After the famine of the third seal, who knows what the food supply will be like, and there may not be much food from the sea used anymore. Depending on what news reporting will be like, the world's population may not ever know ships were destroyed.

The third trumpet has a great star falling from heaven and making a third of the rivers and springs of water bitter (Revelation 8:10-11). Many men will die from the lack of good drinking water. Satan may not have to do much with this sign because death will be so common in the Tribulation. He may just reason this away as the undesirables dying to keep more resources for those who deserve to live.

The fourth trumpet strikes the sun, moon and stars, drastically changing how much light is given during the day and night (Revelation 8:12). Satan may attribute this sign to climate change, which is a lie being propagated today. Beyond climate change, there are organizations who are openly experimenting with blocking out the sun to parts of the earth. Satan could explain this was an experiment helping those who still live on the earth. Satan could also blame all people for their activities that are killing the earth and use it as a means to increase control over earth's resources just like governments are doing today.

We discussed the firth trumpet—the locusts—during the chapter on demons and their characteristics (Revelation 9:1-11). The demons described as locusts will harm all unbelievers for five months. Satan may use this as another opportunity to blame believers and Jews for all the troubles in the world which would give him more power to kill them. This is one of the three woes mentioned in Revelation and will be very painful for unbelievers so much they will wish to die but won't be allowed. Much like the sixth seal, I do not know how Satan will use this sign for his deception, but he will certainly find a way.

The sixth trumpet has angels killing a third of mankind through fire, smoke, and brimstone (Revelation 9:13-19). If the population of the earth is about eight billion as it is now when the Tribulation starts, through only this trumpet and the fourth seal, four billion people are going to be killed. That is half of the starting population in less than three and a half years, which doesn't even count the death from the other seals and trumpets. Death will be extremely common place during the Tribulation. Satan may try to "normalize" death so much people don't contemplate why so many are dying.

After this trumpet is described, John says, "And they did not repent of their murders or their sorceries or their sexual immorality or their thefts" (Revelation 9:21). This may indicate the sorceries, which is the word *pharmekeia*, and sexual immorality offer people just enough comfort from the terrible pain of the locusts and massive amounts of death so that they still do not seek the real Savior. The murders, which may lead to cannibalism because of the lack of food, and thefts also sustain people to stay alive since resource shortages will probably continue past the third seal. Whatever way Satan and the Antichrist deceive people, they will still be led to worship them instead of God.

Chapter 46

Deception of the Bowls

The first bowl brings a foul and loathsome sore upon all unbelievers (Revelation 16:2). Satan may try to deceive the world into thinking this a virus spreading throughout the earth and the only way to stop the rising number of cases is to institute lock downs for all people. There may also be mask mandates or any number of other counter measures to combat the "virus." These restrictions, of course, won't work because the sores are coming from God's wrath, not anything man has done.

The second bowl turns the sea into blood and every sea creature will die (Revelation 16:3). Demons may try to copy this sign as they did with the second trumpet, but the sheer magnitude of all the oceans of the world turning to blood will not be able to be copied just as the magicians of Egypt were not able to copy the lice (Exodus 8:18-19). As we said before, we don't know how much food will be coming from the sea, so mankind's food supply may not be altered too much from this sign. However, the destruction of the largest ecosystem on the planet will have devastating effects of every other animal still living. Yet Satan will most likely have a deception ready to give the world for how everything will be fine as long as they keep worshiping himself and the Antichrist.

As if turning the oceans into blood wasn't enough, the third bowl turns the freshwater of the earth into blood (Revelation 16:4). Satan and the Antichrist will have a plan to feed and quench the thirst of the people they still want alive. Maybe they will have stored enough water to survive for a little while, but one would think these two bowls happen close to the end of the Tribulation. With no source of clean water, how long could people survive if there is not a large stockpile of things to drink?

Through God's judgments, especially the last two, the Antichrist may develop a system in which people are rewarded with life giving supplies for their allegiance and service to him. Maybe the only way to get water and food, without God's intervention, is to get the mark of the beast? Maybe more food from the Antichrist's cache is awarded to a soldier who catches a believer and puts them to death? By this point in the seven year period, conditions to sustain life will be so extreme people will probably do just about anything to survive.

The fourth bowl is poured on the sun and the angel who poured it is given power to scorch men with fire and heat (Revelation 16:8-9). Satan's deception for this bowl may include an explanation of solar flares or climate change eroding the Earth's atmosphere so that it no longer protects people from the sun's rays. It doesn't look as if there is much protection for unbelievers from this bowl, and they will blaspheme God instead of giving Him glory.

The next bowl fills the Antichrist's kingdom with darkness (Revelation 16:10-11), probably in a similar way to when Egypt was filled with darkness during the ninth plague (Exodus 10:21-23). Pain from the darkness will be so great unbelievers will gnaw at their tongues. They probably will also still be recovering from the burns of the fourth bowl.

Both the fourth and fifth bowl mention men not repenting of their deeds and blaspheming the name of God (Revelation 16:9, 11). Satan may not even need to provide a lie by this point, because men are so stubborn in their ways they will not turn from worshiping the Antichrist and Satan. How sad that even after God's wrath on them is so great, they do not believe in Jesus as their Savior.

The sixth bowl dries up the Euphrates river so that the kings from the east can travel to Armageddon to prepare for the final battle with Jesus (Revelation 16:12-16). Whatever armaments the kings have might not be able to cross the river, so the dried river bed will enable them to travel to the battle site. Three unclean spirits go out of the mouth of Satan, the Antichrist, and the false prophet to gather the kings for battle. After the darkness and sores from the heat, direct intervention from demons may be the only way to get the soldiers to move from the east. Through all of this, the city of Babylon will most likely be the center of the Antichrist's kingdom. As the kings from the east travel to Armageddon, it is likely they will witness the destruction of the city of Babylon at the pouring of the final bowl.

The seventh bowl is poured in the air and the earth is massively changed (Revelation 16:17-21). There will be great storms of thunder and lighting, a massive earthquake exceeding the measurements of the Richter scale, Babylon will be divided and fall as will many other cities, islands will be moved, and mountains will no longer be mountains. The earth will no longer look like the earth we know today. Furthermore, there will be a great hailstorm, probably killing people and destroying most if not all of whatever is left of their settlements. Yet Antichrist's hold on people will be so great they will still blaspheme God and march to the battle of Armageddon.

Through all of these amazing signs performed by God, the

Deceiving by Signs

Antichrist will still control a large enough army to make them think they can defeat Him. This shows an amazing allegiance to this man beyond what we may see today to any political figure. While I have given a few examples of what the deceptions might be during the Tribulation, I'm sure there are many I have not thought of. However, my intent has not been to exhaustively guess what Satan and the Antichrist might say or do to get people to follow them, mostly because Scripture does not give us the answer. In fact, ten years after this book is published, there may be a whole other set of deceptions we might guess would appear in the Tribulation. God has not revealed these details to us, but He has given us His Word with which to test all things and hold fast to what is good (I Thessalonians 5:21). Whatever we experience as we grow closer to the Rapture and Tribulation should be examined in the light of Scripture to know whether it is a deception from Satan or not. Satan's doctrine is powerfully persuasive, but by taking up the shield of faith we are able "to quench all the fiery darts of the wicked one" (Ephesians 5:16).

Conclusion

One of the biggest lessons I've learned from writing about and researching the topic of power, signs, and lying wonders in both the Bible and modern life is this: people are very impressed and drawn to signs and wonders we cannot explain. For example, we see a light in the sky not matching a natural explanation, and we think it has some great significance or we seek to have that experience again. The interest in the supernatural is increasing during our modern era and will most likely keep increasing until Jesus returns.

Satan and his demons are capable of what I would call "parlor tricks;" they give a human knowledge they couldn't have by normal means, they move an object, they appear as lights in the sky, etc. Why are we so impressed by these cheap imitations compared to God's power? God will not do little tricks for us to satisfy our supernatural wants. He uses His power to glorify His Name and we cannot compel Him to do any sign or wonder just because we think we want or need something. On the other hand, Satan and his demons are very happy to oblige human's wants by giving them some supernatural sign to satisfy their desire and deceive them away from God. How sad that we are content with such inferior displays of power just to satisfy our taste for the supernatural.

Isaiah 64:4 comes to mind: "For since the beginning of the world men have not heard nor perceived by the ear, nor has the eye seen any God besides You, Who acts for the one who waits for Him." Paul quoting this verse in I Corinthians 2:9 says it this way: "Eye has not seen, nor ear heard, nor have entered into the heart of man the things which God has prepared for those who love Him." Even though we can look at the glorious creation God has made or see His power throughout the Bible and miracles He is still doing today, we cannot even conceive of what He has prepared for us in heaven. Why then, would we look for signs from demons we can currently see when God's signs from the past are greater and we cannot imagine what He will do in the future?

Isaiah 64:5 concludes the previous verse this way: "You meet him who rejoices and does righteousness, who remembers You in Your ways. You are indeed angry, for we have sinned— In these ways we continue; and we need to be saved." While this verse is talking about Israel's sin, are we any different? If we are not doing righteousness, is God going to meet us with His blessing? Are we seeking supernatural experiences apart from God because we are not being fulfilled by Him? And if we are not being fulfilled by Him, is it God's fault or ours?

"Humble yourselves in the sight of the Lord, and He will lift you up" (James 4:10). When we spend time with God, whether it is praying, reading the Bible, singing, or any other activity, He will draw near to us because we are drawing near to Him (James 4:8). When we turn away from Satan's influence and power, God will fill us with His own to do amazing things for His glory.

One last observation about the growing influence of Satan and demons' power is if people are drawn to the supernatural, then it can become a topic of conversation. If you are talking about supernatural signs and wonders to an unbeliever, it becomes an opportunity to talk about the greatest sign that ever occurred: "Christ died for our sins according to the Scriptures, and that He was buried, and that He rose again the third day according to the Scriptures" (I Corinthians 15:3-4). We should always look for ways to share the Gospel because we want all people to believe in that sign rather than any deceptive signs.

I hope this book has been enjoyable to read. Hopefully, you now have a better foundation with which to recognize deceptive power, signs, and lying wonders as we grow closer to the Rapture and Tribulation.

Thank you for reading and God bless you!

About the Author

Lucas is a bondservant of Jesus Christ.

www.ingramcontent.com/pod-product-compliance
Lightning Source LLC
Chambersburg PA
CBHW030256100526
44590CB00012B/417